LOVE

LOVE is patient,

love is kind.

It does not envy,

it does not boast,

it is not proud.

It is not rude,

it is not self-seeking,

it is not easily angered,

it keeps no record of wrongs. Love does

not delight in evil but

rejoices with the truth.

It always protects,

always trusts,

always hopes,

and always perseveres.

Love never fails.

But where there are prophecies,

they will cease;

where there are tongues,

they will be stilled;

where there is knowledge,

it will pass away.

1 Corinthians 13:4-8

Testimonials

'Our friendship began when I met Luciane on a bus and began chatting to her approximately six years ago. She is a strong, friendly, warm-hearted woman. I supported Luciane as best I could when she was going through her marriage difficulties and today I see Luciane has grown emotionally and continues to shine and bless others around her! She has the capacity and passion to help women who may be struggling in life as Luciane herself has overcome challenges and grown stronger.'

– **Kim Artery**

'Luciane has helped me in making crucial decisions at various stages in my life. She is a gifted listener and brings clarity and harmony to a situation.'

– **Bree Francisco**

'Before I met Luciane I was living in shame and fear. I had not spoken to my extended family or friends about what was happening at home. When someone saw a glimpse of bad behaviour from my partner, I would make excuses for him. Luciane shared her story with me and gave me support and encouragement. I now live free from the cycle of abuse. Luciane taught me that it is never too late to show your children what behaviour to accept in a relationship. I am on the road to recovery and look forward to reading this book.'

– **Donna Cook, Nurse,**
Central Coast/NSW

'Over the past two years since Luciane first engaged with our service, I have observed during her appointments that she is a patient and dedicated mother, who encourages her daughter Joahnne to learn. She has always gone out of her way to thank me for our support, and has demonstrated that she is trying to make a better life for both herself and Joahnne. She has displayed strength and resilience as a survivor of domestic violence and has the potential to advocate and support other women who are experiencing domestic or family violence.'

– Jade Churchill

NILS Coordinator, Gosford City No Interest Loans Scheme, Gosford/Narara Community Centre

'I had the privilege of getting to know Luciane over the past year as we shared the "Recovery" journey. Her bright and happy personality was infectious and she brought a sense of joy despite the difficulties she faced in life. Luciane had a very strong commitment to personal growth and worked very hard at examining herself and then was willing to make the necessary hard choices to make life work in a healthier way for herself and her daughter. Underpinning all of this was a deep dependence on the power of Christ to enable her to love, forgive and maintain healthy boundaries. Part of her journey is the writing of her story in this book and I am sure it will be a blessing to many.'

– Dr Mary Wood

"Celebrate Recovery" Facilitator.

'When I spoke to Luciane to share my situation, I didn't imagine how much she could guide me. After a few conversations and confidences exchanged, I realised how important it is to have someone who already walked the path you are just starting. Luciane encouraged me to seek help, she showed the way and steps to be taken and who to talk with. I now realised how significant it is when we are able to regain control of our lives.'

– Vanina Ferreira Pierozzi

'A sisterhood for life ... so we were presented spiritually for almost 20 years ago. Luciane is a true and fair person who believes in life, in people, in love and justice. Enlightened people are like that! When Australia entered her plans, for almost 10 years, destiny sent her to Sydney, where she married, had her sweet daughter and lived through the battle and theme of this book: a story of challenges, fears, rejection, humiliation, detachment, understanding and finally overcoming. Be happy is one constant pursuit of all, but sometimes life presents to us the difficulties necessary to challenge our capacity of strength and love, just to teach us that happiness is already in us. But yet in hard times, to count on the support of someone experienced can be the big difference on achieving success.'

– **Andrea Schilling**

'Luciane, I have to thank you, your positive attitude and problem solving is inspiring. I also have had a bad time with my divorce while being in a new country with my four children and very little money. I have survived this due to the support of many wonderful people, from all socioeconomic levels, religions and cultures. Where everyone has experienced some sort of hardship, and has made it through, and then has chosen not to forget but grow and share their new knowledge. I did not break; I did not lose my sanity but filled myself with hope, patience, acceptance rather than fear of the unknown. Different does not have to be bad, different is just different, and finally trust, not only in myself but the universe, God, and all the new people who came along to help. Like you. You have provided me with such important information to overcome little obstacles like how to contact a moving company for free to the massive job of making an effort to spread the word about my situation in order to make a difference for the next to come. And mostly your very constant wise words from the heart, I feel close to you without ever meeting in person, and I already know I will never forget you and you are such an inspiration and you are part of my motivation to give to others my acquired knowledge after this crisis to help others once I finally come out.'

– **Ivonne Henriquez**

'Thanks for everything you have done ... you are such sweet and selfless person. Thanks for helping to get Ivonne's story out there and be an angel for her and her kids.'

– Maria Del Carmen

'Luciane is a true friend and an absolute believer in her truth about how women can survive and thrive after domestic violence. What I love about Lucy is that she is undeterred, intelligent, generous and thoughtful. Her determination to provide a better life for her daughter meant persisting in the struggle to get answers in a foreign country and navigate the system to finally be able to stand on her own two feet. Her young daughter is a credit to her, she is lively and grounded whilst being incredibly mature for her age. It has been such a joy to know Lucy and I am so proud of her for writing this book, because I know that what she has to say has come from somewhere deep inside her, and will support other women in the transition to searching for a better life.'

– Tiffany Burton
Eden Energy Medicine Practitioner

'For as long as I've know Luciane, she's always been positive and enthusiastic, the crises she has had to endure has given her more strength and determination to go on. She has overcome negativity and hardship with such strength that she has burst through with more light in her heart that I ever thought possible in a person. Through all this hardship she has remained a strong and courageous mother and has passed all her love and fight for what's right onto her darling daughter. Her amazing strength as a woman and a mother can be felt immediately when you are in her presence and I know her words of experience and the wisdom in this book will be beneficial to anyone with self doubt or needing a little lift of heart.'

– Amanda Lieber

'I have had the fortunate opportunity to have been Luciane's counsellor at the Central Coast Community Women's Health Centre at Wyoming on the NSW Central Coast. Over recent months that Luciane and I have worked together I have been witness to Luciane's courageous journey in the recovery from her abusive relationship, the rediscovery of herself, her authentic self and the associated challenges of such a situation, from parenting to remaining financially afloat to regaining hope for the future and in fact mapping out what that new future may look like.

'Luciane approached this crisis of a lifetime always with a willingness to learn, to look honestly at the things that are often the most painful to look at and always, with an often hard to find under these types of circumstances, compassion, warmth and humor. I wish her well and all the blessings on the next leg of her life's journey.'

– Julie Darge

Counsellor/Group Facilitator,
Central Coast Community Women's Health Centre

Touched by Love

Turning Crisis into a Blessing

First published by Busybird Publishing 2016
Copyright © 2016 Luciane Sperling

ISBN
Print: 978-0-9953503-6-6
Ebook: 978-0-9953503-7-3

Luciane Sperling has asserted her right under the Copyright, Designs and Patents Act 1988 to be identified as the author of this work. The information in this book is based on the author's experiences and opinions. The publisher specifically disclaims responsibility for any adverse consequences, which may result from use of the information contained herein. Permission to use information has been sought by the author. Any breaches will be rectified in further editions of the book.

All rights reserved. No part of this publication may be reproduced, stored in or introduced into a retrieval system, or transmitted in any form, or by any means (electronic, mechanical, photocopying, recording or otherwise) without the prior written permission of the author. Any person who does any unauthorised act in relation to this publication may be liable to criminal prosecution and civil claims for damages. Enquiries should be made through the publisher.

Cover image: Kev Howlett, Busybird Publishing]
Cover design: Busybird Publishing
Layout and typesetting: Busybird Publishing
Editor: Blaise van Hecke

Busybird Publishing
PO Box 855
Eltham Victoria
Australia 3095
www.busybird.com.au

Contents

Acknowledgements	i
Foreword	v
Introduction	vii
Chapter 1 – Touched by the Past	1
Chapter 2 – Touched by Crisis	25
Chapter 3 – Touched by Awareness	41
Chapter 4 – Touched by Reality	53
Chapter 5 – Touched by Love	61
Chapter 6 – Touched by Decision	69
Chapter 7 – Touched by Community	87
Chapter 8 – Touched by Growth	97
Chapter 9 – Touched by Faith	107
Chapter 10 – Touched by Forgiveness	119
Chapter 11 – Touched by Gratitude	129
Chapter 12 – Touched by Recovery	135
Afterword	143
Touching your Senses	145
Resources and Support – Getting Connected	151
Sponsors and Non-profit Partners	159
Appendices	163
Safety Checklist	165
Safety Strategies	165
Diagrams	170
About the Author	177
About My Inner Light	179
Connecting with Luciane	181
Special Bonus	185

Dedication

This book is dedicated with deep love to my beautiful daughter Joahnne, who has been my biggest strength and my biggest why to overcome each one of our life challenges, my lighthouse on our journey and the greatest gift I could ever receive. I am so blessed to be chosen to be her mother, receiving the chance to live this life adventure with her. She is my strength and the light of my path. My prayer is that I would always honour this gift, being just the mum she needs me to be.

This book is dedicated to you, the woman that backs herself with strength and pride. The one who stands up in the storm with a smile on her face, she knows in her heart that her darkest days, no matter how hard they are, are only the sign of showing her how to push further into her inner light, to be able to see wisdom and opportunity hidden in it. To the woman who will always conquer her milestones with grace, beauty and honour.

Love & Light,

Luciane Sperling.

*'Ladies, most of you have no idea how beautiful you are.
Don't let mean words from an
insecure soul blind you from
the truth of your beauty.
You are beautiful by design ...
Just the way you are.'*
– Steve Maraboli

Acknowledgements

I would like to express my gratitude to the many friends who will always be acknowledged in my heart, for kindly spending their time while giving me their hand to overcome many challenges through recent years. I am always grateful, they know who they are!

I would like to thank from my heart for the sweet testimonials received while writing this book, your words and kindness touched my heart. And thanks to each one of you who ordered this book when in pre-sales campaign; you all made me believe.

I would like to thank my sponsors, which without them it would not be possible to bring this book to reality. My special gratitude goes to Melissa Polwarth who I can't thank enough.

I must show deep gratitude to the supporter's organisations listed below. Without receiving their grace I would not be able to feel safe and provide all the needs and the best life possible for my daughter, while rebuilding life from times of financial challenges and emotional crisis.

I would like to thank Natasa and Stuart Denman for adopting me to their Ultimate 48Hour Author family, for pushing me through mentoring and coaching causing me to became a published author in Australia. Thank you Busybird Publishing who encouraged me when issues arose on meeting our deadlines and thank you Nikola Boskovski, who worked after hours to deliver the illustrations to beautify this book.

And in saying that, I want to thank all those who provided support, talked things over, reading, writing, offering comments, creating tools for promotion, allowed me to quote their remarks and assisted in the editing, proofreading and design. I can't thank enough my friend Tiffany Burton for pushing me harder to achieve deadlines and I must also show gratitude to Simone Wylie and Sallie-Ann Macklin, Jenny Phare, Hamish Bruce, Tony Park.

A special thank you to my family despite living miles away, always found a manner to show their care and love towards me and their grand-daughter Joahnne.

A special gratitude goes to the force of the universe, which I call God, and that always shows solutions to provide what I deserve to receive.

Last and not least, I beg forgiveness of all those who have been with me over the course of the years and whose names I have failed to mention here, but will be always in my memory.

You all touched my heart with kindness and love, walking me from crisis to blessing:

Brighter Futures Program – Annabel Rees

CCFSS Family Support Gosford – Wendy Gane

Central Coast Community Women's Health Centre

Central Coast Family Support

Centrelink Department of Human Services

Coast Shelter Gosford – Charles

Cominos Lawyers Sydney – Pamela Cominos

EV Church Erina

Family Relationship Centre – Northern Beaches

Impact Centre and Church Erina

Liberty Life House – Gosford

Lighthouse Single Mothers – Dee Why

Link Housing NSW

Manly Warringah Women's Resource Centre

Narara Neighbourhood Community Centre – Jade Churchill

Northside Community Connect – Reg Barlow

Pregnancy Help Manly Warringah – Margarete

Relationships Australia
Seed of Light Brookvale
St Vincent de Paul Society – Gosford / Brookvale
The Salvation Army – Brookvale / Lane Cove / Collaroy
The Salvation Army Gosford – Kristy Fell
Women's Refuge Bringa Dee Why – Narelle Hand
Women's Refuge Delvena Lane Cove – Melanie Lovelock

'Sometimes in life, you find a special friend;
someone who changes your life just by being part of it.
Someone who makes you laugh until you can't stop;
someone who makes you believe on the best of the world;
someone who convinces you that there
really is an unlocked door just waiting for you to open it'
-Unknown

Foreword

'With everything that has happened to you, you can either feel sorry for yourself or treat what has happened as a gift. Everything is either an opportunity to grow or an obstacle to keep you from growing. You get to choose.'

– Wayne Dyer

When I first met Luciane Sperling she stood out as a person of strength, heart and passion. Luciane's story is one of courage, commitment, compassion and extraordinary resilience. Writing her story is an act of bravery and symbolic of Luciane's dedication to the principle that all people have the right to dignity and respect. *Touched by Love* explores one person's struggle, to ensure the right for herself and her daughter, and also her spiritual and personal growth, which she will share with the readers.

Luciane will take you on a journey from alienation through the passage of trauma to an eventual life of freedom, authenticity and abundance. I am blessed to know Luciane as a friend. It is a joy and pleasure to know her and to share with her about her dreams and what the future holds for her.

The best is yet to come for you my friend! Thank you for being you and for making the difference to so many people.

– **Nada Potter,**
President Chertseydale Cottage
President KDO 2016

Introduction

There are times in life where we can find ourselves living in such odd situations where the unthinkable happens, and where we feel there is no way out to the road of hope. This book is primarily about love, universal love, but also about crisis and how important it is to be able to view opportunities and blessings hidden behind our broken feelings. We all came into this world with a spiritual mission to learn and grow through connecting with people throughout our journey. I believe people come to our life for a reason and they are intentionally presented into our world with the purpose of growth, while experiencing how to deal with challenging circumstances between us. From the Creator, we received this gift of an amazing chance to make life better with each other if facing our real weakness and fears, by experiencing pain and healing, achieving spiritual freedom, which will allow us to finally succeed at being ourselves in our full potential.

This book has no intention to be an autobiography but is about my personal story of love and pain and my journey of growth through it while struggling to navigate and survive into a completely new world being quickly unravelled, and also while being a lovingly, busy and very dedicated mother. How I could, at some point be able to see things wisely from another angle, when I took myself emotionally out of the situation and faced my reality. I learnt that other people's journey does not belong to me, and yet more important, had to mentor myself again to value and respect my core values. It is about finding blessings through the crisis and feeling grateful for the learning and grateful for the people who were meant to be in this process.

Crisis can be considered as any event if it wipes out your ability to make sense out of what is happening. You may feel helpless and the victim of events beyond your control and expectations. The unexpected does create uncertainty and fear and is seen as a threat to your dreams and goals. Yet the crisis can be reduced to something manageable when we regain good sense of understanding and self control through the ability of training your mind to see those events with different emotions.

That is when you find blessings. Blessings are signs to the faithful of the spiritual benefits achieved through the act of giving thanks; see the beauty and find joy and happiness in the middle of a hard time ... this is a gift from God.

I hope that you, the reader, will be able to find your blessings through the crisis situations you may be living right now. Any challenge that would be dragging you to the point of feeling hopeless is actually your unique chance of opportunity to overcome it all, making better decisions and choices for your life and finally being able to find yourself living the purpose you really were called for, even before you arrived in this world.

> 'The light within can elevate us to heights we've never dreamed possible. Once you realize that God, the Light, the infinite intelligence, whatever you want to call it, is inside you, you will realize, like I have, that nothing is impossible.'
>
> – Wayne Dyer

Chapter 1
Touched by the Past

'Your past has given you the strength and wisdom you have today, so celebrate it. Don't let it haunt you. Your past mistakes are meant to guide you, not define you.'

– **John Baker,** *Celebrate Recovery*

Do you know that your current feelings, your personality traits and your current behaviours are shaped by the past events you've been through? Do you know that all the experiences that you've been through as a little child are profoundly impacting your life right now, even the events that might seem irrelevant or insignificant? Do you know that your past experiences are currently affecting your present and that it will keep affecting your future as long as you don't become aware of the connection between the present, your past and your future? To understand your present, it is really important to understand the impact of the past, so you can have the power to change your future, avoiding so many mistakes that affect and hurt the people around you, especially the closest ones who love you.

It is June 2016, and I am sitting under a beautiful autumn tree at the playground watching my beautiful daughter Joahnne running and playing, excited, happy and healthy. We have been living in the beautiful Central Coast for exactly three years now, and our life is about to change again. We are moving to a better place to live and this book is about to be launched. We have such an incredible bond built through the last seven years, based in trust, harmony, loyalty, difficulties faced together with happiness and a profound love. We are connected by soul as we can easily "feel" and "read" each other's feelings and emotions. We have been through a lot of different experiences together since she was a little baby and our life journey has deeply connected us. This magical time of the year is bringing colourful displays from the deciduous trees here in New South Wales. They are my favourite trees. The shaped leaves turn into brilliant hues of red, gold, rust and orange, showing the nature's ability to change and adapt, as each one of us living on this beautiful earth. The branches sound like a music softly against the breeze. It is cold like a crocodile's back and we can smell amber around the air. The branches appearing to extend their arms to reach the sun and I can see a Jacky Winter sitting upright on a bare branch, wagging its tail from side to side and uttering its 'peter peter' call. There are enough leaves on the pathway to walk on our way home. It is winter in Australia, and if you are visiting Sydney you must make sure to join a whale-watching cruise departing from Circular Quay, or go for one of the many scenic coastal walks. If you are more adventurous, you may try climbing the Sydney Harbour Bridge. It is a blessed and beautiful country that Joahnne and I call home.

But, how did I get here? Looking back 10 years, when I arrived in Australia for the first time, I wouldn't ever guess that one day I was going to share my life story of courage, happiness, blessings, love, achievements but also the story of biggest challenges, crisis, trauma, brokenness, and then growth, forgiveness, gratitude and recovery based strongly in faith. I could not imagine that one day I would use my hardship experience to support women and their children, lighting awareness about abusive relationships, and more important, on how to bring your own inner light back to you, if you recognise that you are in one. So, grab a cup of tea or a glass of wine and follow this journey with me. I hope you will feel touched by love yourself.

Arriving in Australia

It was 21st September 2006, and I could already see the Australian coast from the air. I had the happy feeling of pinching myself while still feeling the warmest farewell ever with my family and closest friends back in Brazil. The plan of migrating to Australia commenced just some months before when I decided that I wanted to live in a more developed country to study English, learn new skills and live and work in a safer environment with access to higher quality life. A place with new opportunities and where I would culturally identify myself better with the values I have. At the beginning I was planning Canada, but then changed my mind to Australia. To make my plan work, I decided to sell my home, car, and close my conference business plus give away all my belongings to my sisters, brothers and friends and finally packing two suitcases and a heart filled with faith, giving my destiny in God's hands.

I still remember the moment I told my father Danilo about my decision. We were at the church and he said, 'Darling, just don't sell your home.' I replied, 'I sold it already!' When it was time to leave my place for the new owner, I spent two days with friends until the big day of departing. I have in my memory the day my father came to my home and there were boxes everywhere, and seeing that scene brought tears to his eyes. His wife, my stepmother Maria Cleia, told me later that when he returned home that night, he was breaking down in tears, fearing for me but he was also very happy and proud. At that time my father and I were so close, we were bonded together in friendship. He was so different from the father of my childhood as he had grown so much in understanding, compassion, empathy and love through the church. He had come from crisis years to blessing years in his life and in our relationship. He could find blessings in everything in his life, and relate to life and to people in a much healthier way, especially with his three daughters and son. My mother Jane was also worrying about me as any mother would be, but very happy and excited about my moving to Australia. My mother lived in Brazil in a distant city, and we would speak to each other frequently. She experienced an overwhelming number of difficulties and traumatic events through her life and was faithful and resilient enough to turn it all into blessings through the years. My mum is a very strong women and also very kind and giving. I am proud to say that my parents are friends and it means a lot to me.

I suppose I make it sound easy, just selling everything and coming to Australia, but in reality it wasn't easy at all and required lots of research and planning. I was leaving behind not just assets and everything I already had achieved professionally, but also quite a good life surrounded with good friends sharing the same values, a very nice social life due to my conference business, prestige, respectful career connections, church, and most of all my family, especially my grandmother Arlinda. Starting fresh from zero again, leaving all that I had and all that I knew behind, and focusing my mind just on the enormous possibilities of adventures, and new achievements – my new life ahead at 37 years old. I left my home with my courage and a heart filled with dreams!

My luck already sparkled like a diamond when I was flying to Sydney, as I met a friend who was flying back from visiting his family in Brazil. He not only lived in Sydney but yet in the same complex I was going to live! He was very kind and offered to take the same taxi to go home. Little did I know he was going to turn into a best friend and guide, my trusty brother in heart, especially during the first year or two and then through the worst moments of crisis and desperate situations that I was going to face a few years later. The apartment complex was located at Alexandria, 20 minutes from Sydney by train and I loved the place. It was a secure complex with quite modern buildings and I was sharing with other Brazilian students. I shared a room with a friend called Roberta and I was very lucky to have a flatmate with the same values. The other room was shared between three boys, all cousins and also from Brazil.

The first three months I was exclusively attending school to study English. I arrived in Australia with basic American English, as my father provided private English classes when I was in high school. But I'll tell you Mate, studying Australian English is harder, specially the pronunciation. I was also exploring Sydney and enjoying making new friends from all over the world. After graduating in English classes at Carrick Institute, it was time to start the professional Events Management course I was already enrolled in before arriving in Australia. But I realised that the Events Management course wouldn't allow me to apply for Australian residency in the future. And that was the whole point. So I quickly changed my course to Hospitality Management Advanced Diploma (Patisserie) and of course I had to pay much more money for that. It was a very expensive course and I studied two years full-time. I was working as a conference and events waitress for four different companies: Westin Sydney Resort, Sydney Convention Centre, Luna Park and the Sydney Opera House. I was working very hard and studying full time. I had a very busy and tight schedule between jobs, with no time for anything else, but I was working to reach my goals and felt very blessed and happy.

Love knocking at the front door

One Friday night in December, after one of my late jobs finished at the Sydney Opera House, I was at the bus stop waiting for my bus to return home, listening to good music, while watching perplexed as so many young people were drunk on the streets after going to parties. Anyway, a girlfriend of mine who also was living in my building was walking with a friend to the bus stop. But my eyes were already on her friend before I even realised that she was walking with him. I still remember thinking to myself, *Hmm ... that's a gorgeous man.* His physical appearance with grey hair, light-brown skin, fleshy lips, with a charming walk, looked attractive to me. Much later, I realised that his physical appearance was quite similar to one of my ex-boyfriends, who had been a significant part of my life. In my sub-conscious, the attraction was connected to the feelings of happiness, love and safety and the main message was the feeling of 'trust' because of the emotional memory from that relationship of the past.

As quickly as I met his eyes, I turned my eyes away to avoid embarrassment but before I knew it, they both came walking towards me! My friend touched my shoulder and *he* was introduced to me, and straight away we had made an emotional connection. That was the first time we met, but couldn't even guess that he was going to be my future husband. We got on the same bus to go home. We were visibly attracted to each other but I decided to deny it. The next day he asked my girlfriend for my phone number and he started some calls. . I found him emotionally attractive too. But I thought that I shouldn't have a relationship with a Brazilian man as I was expecting to build a family in Australia. I had no doubts that Australia was my new home. I also wished my future kids to have the opportunity to at least have half of their extended family in Australia. All of my family were in Brazil. My grandparents were so significant in my life, and I wanted my kids to have the gift of Australian grandparents living close to them. I remember talking to myself in front of the mirror, trying to avoid thinking about a possibility of having a relationship with this man. It was like my mind and my heart were having a discussion. He looked older than me, so I assumed he was, as maturity was an important characteristic for me in order to be with a man. Unfortunately this wasn't the case, and it was shown through his future actions and reactions. But now, red flags like that don't matter right? When we are in love and blinded, eluded by the image the person is willing to show us we just believe in what we are being shown.

I know I have a very strong intuition, my senses work in synergy and I trust them; I can really "read" people's energy and really feel them from inside. This time my intuition *was* triggered but I let myself be carried by his demonstrations of heartfelt love for me, and in a way I wanted to feel it too. Little did I know that soon I would get to know his other face, other side, other scary man inside, and that my concept of love and family was totally different from his knowledge about love. Even though my intuition to avoid him was still in my mind, I continued living my life as normal, and I had the opportunity to have one of the most beautiful New Years Eve to begin 2007. I joined some friends to sail on a boat while watching the Sydney Harbour Bridge exploding in fireworks just above my eyes. Not knowing the danger of sharks around, after the 9pm fireworks, we decided to swim in the harbour. Now that is something to remember. I had such a lovely birthday dinner in January at the Sydney Tower. Sometimes I would go out and meet my girlfriends Jackie, Lana and Karyne. They were guaranteed to make me laugh, they were not so serious as I was, and I was having the best time of my life.

A short time later, meeting up with this seeming charming man became quite regular as, to my surprise, he was working at the student agency I was having appointments to solve my study decisions. He was calling and messaging romantic messages all the time, and he became really determined to get my attention with his charm and charisma, making me feel so special, cared for and desired by him. We started dating seriously in July 2007, on his birthday, and it was then that I found out he was eight years younger than me. At that time I decided to ignore this first red flag, and I still have the email I wrote to my family in August telling them I was in love and in a relationship, speaking a little about him and how he won my heart and trust.

Before I allowed myself to be more emotionally involved, I decided to have a serious conversation with him about Australia and Brazil and our real expectations. It happened in Coogee, in front of the beach, watching the ocean from the hill. I had come to Australia to stay, and he had come to Australia to study English and return. So, I thought that I must be clear with him about my intentions, because if he didn't want to stay in Australia, it was better to break up now to avoid a future conflict of interest. He said that he had decided to stay in Australia, and since then we began an intense and passionate relationship filled with emotions and deep connections. He was always sending love messages, love callings, assurance of fidelity and passion and being very protective and romantic, ticking all the boxes I needed emotionally. Our friends were always saying how we looked like a perfect happy couple. I poured out my heart to him, and he was pouring out his heart to me. We had so much fun and adventures together, very special and romantic moments and lots of deep conversations.

In October 2007, he had to travel back home to Brazil to attend his brother's wedding and having to part from each other was pretty bloody hard. He had organised a special date in a hotel close to the airport on the night before he was departing, for a night filled with romance. We were so into each other emotionally. It was the best time ever when I felt complete and intensely involved with him who was deeply in love with me. When we were close, the energy would switch to a hot atmosphere and he usually wouldn't keep his hands off me. Making love was profoundly intense and sweet, travelling from a physical to spiritual level of contact, our kisses were always perfect and hot. I knew that such encounters were planned by our souls long before the bodies met each other. That night I gave him a necklace that I had bought when I travelled to Brazil to see my family just a few weeks before. It was one half of a pair of necklaces for couples, with a half heart face each. My half heart was sold in 2011, to be able to pay for needs for our daughter after he left us with nothing when I was forced by the circumstances to leave him the first time.

While he was in Brazil he said he missed me terribly. He wrote one email from Brazil saying that our love had touched his family who saw his joy at having me in his life. And, when calling, he would cry emotionally while talking about his love for me. When he returned from Brazil, we decided to plan a special trip to the Fiji Islands. We were enjoying time together every day. He was very protective and always surrounding me with so much attention and spoiling me all the time. While we were planning our holiday together he decided to get married in Fiji. Because of my belief system and the way I was educated, I asked him to call my father in Brazil and 'ask for my hand' as a sign of respect and consideration with my family to announce our decision, and so he did it, a little shy but politely. Unfortunately, three years later, as the abuse was part of our relationship and he was getting out of his mind and losing control, this very special moment was undermined and sadly denigrated in one of the ugly emails he angrily, and filled with revenge, wrote to my family "giving me back" to my father and saying that "I" was drunk when he had made that call, accusing my family of being a "gang" and also that I was prostitute and many more sad defamations and insults.

When we announced our wedding, my father got a little worried about the short time that we had spent together, which was less than a year. My parents had also fallen deeply in love and were married within a year. Their marriage had been very difficult with a lot of heartache leading to very unhappy ending for their short time together. Although worried, my father was very happy for me, as he knows I wouldn't just go ahead and get married in a foreign country without measuring risks with responsibility. Now of course in hindsight I don't believe I did that very wisely and I understand that I was just about to repeat the relationship patterns of my parents, and little did I know that he was also just about to repeat his parent's relationship pattern with me. No, at that time, I hadn't yet reached this knowledge and I was just intensely living those feelings of being so loved, accepted and cared for, and could easily see myself as his wife and mother of our children. We spoke about having kids on many occasions. I put my trust in him from then on, building our family based on our love, but also based on kindness, honesty, active communication, intimacy, romance, validation, forgiveness, compassion, a mutual desire to achieve goals together and willingness to work through difficulties and disagreements. And in January 2008, just two days before my 39th birthday, we happily got married in Fiji.

Getting Married

Weeks after we started dating, I found out that he was not using his real name. He liked to say that he decided to change his name in Australia because people were not pronouncing his name correctly. At that time I believed, but then I realised he didn't like his name and had found an opportunity to create a new one more charming. I had a strange feeling about it because of double personality but didn't pay serious attention to this red flag as at that time I used to believe everything he said to me, trusting 100%. But it was pretty weird when he didn't like that his name was printed 'wrong' on a wedding gift given to us by a couple that was in our wedding. I was confused when he mentioned that his name was written wrong, because it wasn't, it was his real name. I wanted to please him, so I put my confusion aside and I weirdly agreed with him. Very soon what was initially a romantic holiday to Fiji, somehow turned into an overseas wedding combined with honeymoon. He liked to do things last minute and was unpredictable; rarely planning in advance and was already showing bad time management. So, I excitedly set off planning our wedding using my previous skills as Events Manager when working in Brazil.

I need to feel safe, and being organised provides predictability even yet scheduling a bit of surprises and adventure. In Fiji, we had three days cruising around the islands before heading to our resort, snorkelling under blue waters and walking on paradisiacal beaches. It was magic! We chose to have our marriage celebration in one of the most beautiful boutique hotel retreats in Fiji: Crusoe's Retreat. It was very beautiful, romantic, just the two of us and the hotel's guests. Thinking about our families, I decided to spend extra money and have our celebration recorded on a special movie to send to Brazil.

As all was planned so quickly our families couldn't come from Brazil to be with us at the ceremony. I knew my family would come if there were more time to plan. We had a very traditional Fijian marriage celebration on the beach, neither of us wearing shoes. It was romantic against an unforgettable sunset. I arrived by boat, with a choir singing, and then I was carried by the Fijian warriors on a wedding chair. We had two little flower girls from the village. After the ceremony, we had photos and video making and then I organised a surprise for him: a private small boat to wander around, with a Fijian friend serving champagne and canapés and playing traditional music. We had an immense colourful rainbow on the ocean. We both were having the time of our life, loving deeply each other and dreaming about our future together, home, career, kids, and family. To afford it, I was using my savings account from Brazil and my credit card to pay many of the expenses, as he didn't have a credit card at that time.

Marriage was and still is a very serious matter in my personal values; a wedding ring is a serious commitment. The vows we said to each other, to the wedding celebrant and to God are still printed in my soul, as you will read in chapter 12, Touched by Recovery. These vows still haunt me although I saw them being sadly broken so many times. My parents were divorced when I was about five years old; I have painful memories about that. I have memories of having years craving for love and affection, not sure where I belonged and wishing for a united traditional family if my parents could be working on their issues at that time. Because of that I was very bonded and connected with my grandparents who always made sure to cover me up. I had promised myself to make it different, choosing my husband wisely as I didn't want to risk raising my own future children in a broken family, just as I had been raised. Little did I realise that not only did I marry very quickly just as my parents had, but was going to repeat a similar story of painful separations. And at that time I also wasn't aware about his own family issues pattern, which was going to be huge in the full context. But now I was in love, and any red flags would not be relevant in front of my eyes. If we could have more awareness, our traps could be addressed as soon as arising to succeed.

To me, family means looking after each other with love and compassion, protecting and sticking to each other no matter what. I wanted with all my soul to provide to my future children a healthy, protected and loving environment where mum and dad would be role models, the real meaning of a healthy relationship based in love, mutual respect and filled with open communication to solve family issues, which we, like every other couple, would certainly encounter ahead. I really believed he would sincerely keep all the vows he promised on our wedding day. I married him because at that time he was making me feel safe, cared for, protected, loved, accepted, accountable, respected, and understood. I was both deeply in love and feeling loved enough to get married, even within a short six months dating. He was always communicating with me, listening, looking in my eyes and sharing feelings, anticipating my needs, showing affection and intimacy. To me these were the most important behaviours for the success of a healthy relationship, until they started to disappear, one by one. He was romantic, protective, and charismatic; at that time I had no doubts about my decision. He wasn't wealthy and financially it would be a worry at our age, but I knew we both were starting a new life in a new country. He wouldn't afford the life I used to have or travelling around or other expensive things to impress me, but I had faith we would build it in years, especially after obtaining our Australian permanent residence. I believed he would be the man to provide not just the love I wished for our new family, but also direction, focus, and protection, and that he was going to take care of me and his family forever. I used to have this vision in my mind, seeing us as grandparents, enjoying life together in the future.

Another red flag waved one night on our honeymoon. When speaking about the future I asked him to promise me that he will never go to sleep upset or angry with me, but solve any issues we need to solve before going to sleep. He replied that we will never have this problem because we will never have issues. I remember thinking, *Hmm, I may have trouble here* because adults must cope with disappointment all the time, so I felt the answer as a sign of trouble when hereafter dealing with marriage conflict. But I thought '*Well I will deal with it when it arrives, forget about it now*'. Then a few months after our wedding, I was facing one of the first conflicts of many, where he responded to a simple discussion using the word ' get separated' because 'things weren't going how he expected it would'. At that time I wrote in my diary how disappointed and sad I got and how that did hurt me profoundly. I was starting to feel unsure about what was going to happen in the future. A relatively small conflict had quickly turned into defensiveness, blaming with a hidden threat of 'leaving or stopping loving me', and in his view 'if someone wasn't agreeing with his actions unfortunately doesn't have the same goal so there is no reason to reopen something that would end in different objective' as he handwrote to me on his birthday in 2010. Confused, but I imagined big conflicts in the future, especially as future parents, and realised that our marriage wasn't strongly grounded and looking 'disposable' as like I could be 'returned to my father' at any time for not behaving according to his expectations.

Challenges Arising

We returned to Australia from Fiji, and I had my first difficult time in our love story. The first of our challenges was choosing our new home to live together. Some little conflict was raised but then solved by sweet exchange of mobile messages. I just remember the feeling of not feeling comfortable and a little afraid of upsetting him with my needs. We were still living in separate houses, and after more than a month of searching we finally found a new place to rent and turn it into our home sweet home. I remember one night we were talking about our future and he was showing signs of anxiety about being able to afford a family. While looking for our place we had some disagreement, it was like a subtle mind game using emotions to control my opinion and decision, but of course by that time I considered it 'normal'. To avoid having any disagreement with him and his preferences I agreed with the place he chose instead of the one I liked. But the more important thing was to be happy together, I supposed, putting aside my own opinion about the place.

Before we moved to our place, a second challenge knocked on the door just a week after returning from Fiji. I was at my place when I felt very dizzy and fainted in strong pain. I recalled that when I was in Fiji, I noticed that I was losing blood while having a shower but at the time I didn't realise that I was actually quite ill. My flatmate called him and I was rushed to my doctor who diagnosed an ectopic pregnancy in the last danger stage, which would soon turn into internal bleeding leading to death! It was very big already, ready to explode and a serious life threat. I was referred to the hospital for urgent surgery. That was pretty emotional for us. The nurses felt sorry for us as we had just arrived home from our honeymoon and now losing our baby. So, against the hospital rules, they let him stay with me all night on the hospital bed and the other day I had my left fallopian tube cut out.

After the ectopic pregnancy surgery, I was still recovering and in pain, but we were about to move into our new home from our separate places. I wasn't allowed to carry anything. So I felt very upset when he called to say he was running late and ask me to be ready and I had to bring my own suitcases downstairs. Of course, I didn't feel cared for about my health at this time. When he arrived I wasn't very pleased as the pain was worse because of the effort, and I was hurt because he didn't show empathy or compassion and didn't say anything to make me feel better, but got upset with me because I was showing unpleasant feelings to him. Anyway, we were going to our new home and I just put it aside and I said sorry to him instead! So I was already feeling sorry and trying to help him to feel better, when he was getting upset for not being able to deal with my different opinion or frustrated feeling. In the future we had more and more situations where he reacted badly every time we didn't agree with something, or every time I was showing feelings that he couldn't handle. His reaction was withdrawal, resentment, denial, ignoring, and rejection.

Culturally, we were raised in a very different family environment as his family wasn't wealthy as mine was, so it has lead him to live and experience his life in a very different reality compared with the experiences and reality I was coming from. I was raised in a middle class family environment and I had already achieved some financial and professional goals in my life. I was a mature woman who had already faced negative experiences in a long-term intimate relationship, including being betrayed financially, and had learned some valuable lessons. I was his first seriously committed relationship, giving me the clue that he hadn't had much experience dealing with intimate relationship issues, which was a red flag. I had thought to myself before that in order to avoid future mistakes, I would get married to a man who had already achieved certain emotional maturity and financial security to provide for his family. But I was deeply in love, and I believed that we would learn and achieve everything together, and because he did study accountancy, he would be financially intelligent to protect now 'our' assets.

When we married I had still savings account in Brazil from the sale of my unit and even after investing on my studies and moving to Australia, I had still about AUD$30,000 as well as some savings from working in Australia, which I believed we would increase and use as a deposit for a house one day. My savings started to be used to afford big parts of the wedding, then for things for our new home, then to travel to Hobart on his birthday, then for some expenses travelling to Brazil when I was five months pregnant, then to support him when I stopped working, then to afford baby's needs. I was doing it because I believed that I was supporting him in the beginning while he was doing his best in his capacity to achieve his goals to look after our family. Especially after our baby was born, I was seeing him working a lot at the student agency and also extra shifts at the pizza shop, then in construction sites because he decided to leave the student agency when Joahnne was born. So, I was also financially supporting our life to cover some of expenses using my Brazilian savings account. I wouldn't feel great if not doing it, as I believed that it was what a couple is supposed to do, bring finances together. But I wasn't expecting to spend all the savings I achieved in a lifetime and then being left with nothing in the future, and with a baby to provide. Strangely for me, he never did set up our finances as a couple and had never set any savings plan, financial goals or a joint account so everything my father taught me about long-term financial planning wasn't happening, and I was expecting to trust my husband on leading it to feel safe. When I suggested this he didn't take me seriously, so I thought I would make it work later.

When we moved to our new home in February 2008, I was still recovering from the ectopic pregnancy surgery, finishing my Advanced Diploma in Hospitality and working. We rented out our second room to international students; my husband was working at the student agency, doing airport pickups, and looking after new international students arriving in Australia. We were living as happy as every new couple in love would live, with passion and happiness. He used to call me "my perfect princess", "my endless love", "my goddess", "my little delicious cat" and many other romantic or cute names, numerous emails and mobile messages with promises and affirmations about him falling deeply in love with me again and again for 80 years. So many romantic words, showing his passion desire with the message "I own your soul and you're never getting away and I will take care of you forever" kind of love. As he wrote one day, I was his first.

Between the end of 2008 and during 2009, little more weird situations continued to happen showing something wasn't quite right and I was aware about the domino effect of it. By the middle of 2010, I reckon by the letter I wrote to him on his birthday, that I was getting quite resentful and worried, although not really sharing much so I would not upset him more, preferring to be passive. The events was getting quite repetitive and I knew deep inside that the way we were relating to each other wasn't healthy and that those issues should be urgently addressed, instead of denied. But after each event, the honeymoon phase would always take place, although I never received one single "sorry" for hurting my feelings. I learnt not to pay too much attention and although it was hurting and escalating, I was avoiding confronting or questioning about his choices, much more observing than complaining, and then hopelessly waiting for him to realize what was done and take action. He looked upset if I was sharing my feelings and he wasn't open to hear about it, not knowing what to do with them. Most of our misunderstandings were, at the beginning based on miscommunication or no communication at all, and not sharing or being honestly open about needs and feelings. He would shut down instead of addressing any issues and I would receive back the silent treatment, cold and hot behaviour, defensiveness and blaming, heartless toward me, lack of physical touch or silent treatment. He was choosing the silence to avoid conflict, but wasn't wisely able to see that more pain was being caused because of the silence.

I remember one day I was supposed to go to work but instead I got a bus, and in tears I went to Coogee beach to walk alone trying to figure out what caused one of his first inappropriate reactions. So there I was, sitting on the top of the hill in Coogee, crying out and speaking one hour by the phone with my best friend. When I returned home, I was still feeling deeply sad about the occurrence and expecting we would take action to speak about it and extract a better outcome from this event. When he arrived I was trying to relax in the bath and put my mind in a positive vibe. He opened the door, said 'hi' and acted as if nothing happened, not apologizing nor speaking about the verbal and emotional incident and nothing ever was mentioned about it, seeming to me as I was being punished with his rejection, distance, and withdrawal of love. So again, I sank into myself, healed myself and put a new happy face on. I wasn't even sure if the attitude was calculated to show power control or was his sub-conscious mind starting to control his emotions.

Another event, I organised a special dinner as I used to do every month to celebrate our monthly anniversary. At this time I was already pregnant! It was very special. I planned my afternoon to buy everything and cook for him. It appeared to be all okay, but when the salmon was ready and I invited him to come to the table and open the champagne and light the candles, he asked if I didn't invite the girl that was still renting our spare room. I answered that I already spoke to her about it. The girl didn't usually have dinner with us anyway. But his reaction was so weird and rude; ruining the special moment I planned to make our night special. He got angry with me and when I tried to hug him and say something sweet, he pushed me away and yelled 'I am ashamed to have you as my wife if you do not want to share a plate of food', plus asking if I was jealous of her! I was shocked! Shocked about the physical action of pushing me away from him, the tone of his voice and the hurtful words! I will never forget that situation, because that was the first time the physical abuse occurred. I was really confused and thought, *what is he talking about? Where is that coming from?* So, instead of him feeling happy and grateful for such a nice moment, he was angry and upset and more than that, he was making 'me' feel guilty and blaming me for doing 'something wrong'. Today I know that it's called 'crazy making', which I will explain later in chapter 4, Touched by Reality. That event was pretty sad; the champagne wasn't very nice after all, I went sobbing to our room for some minutes and soon I put myself together and I found myself back in the living room fawning him for us to have dinner and move on. I didn't hear any sorry. And yet, next day, not talking about the issue so I wouldn't make him upset again, better trying to cover it up, as it was his preference. His words and the attitude I received were so hurtful and harsh and made me feel emotionally down and rejected. That wasn't the man I married at all. The attitude was inconsiderate, disrespectful and arrogant with severe and flinty reactions. I couldn't believe he would be able to hurt me with nasty words and heartless kind of attitude.

In October 2009, I kindly wrote four pages about the way he was treating me, the way I was seeing the events happening by now, and was trying to bring awareness to the challenges we were facing and reminding him about our love. I again highlighted that event.

Of course at that time I wasn't able to name and classify the different behaviours as I am able now, and I also didn't know what was causing his changeable moods and what was behind the inability of refusing to share his needs or to be able to have an open, non-judgemental conversation without defensiveness or blockages. I remember my mum used to write letters to my father when she was in a similar situation, so I started to write letters to reach my husband to express my feelings and worries without making him feeling confronted face-to-face and try to help him to open up without fear. I rarely received any feedback either written or spoken. It was all going under the carpet, unsolved, unspoken, faking as though nothing happened and pretending it wasn't there.

My own beliefs around intimate relationships is directly connected with communication and accountability based on respect for each other's feelings. I was raised in a family where we speak out our issues with love and care, respecting and considering with empathy what the other is thinking or feeling, we raise our feelings to the light to solve it and get rid of it, and move on. Later I realised that he was raised in a family where issues aren't able to be solved because they are hidden, negative feelings weren't brought to the light and to still feel accepted and loved. I witnessed some sad events in his family where I saw that happening, but at this time I didn't know it just yet, so I couldn't help him on alerting him about it, so he would maybe realise this pattern and make it different with his wife.

Time passed and I was already walking on shells with him depending on the subject, feeling unsure about his coldness towards me when I "didn't behave well" or when I said something he didn't agree with, and I started to have some uncomfortable feelings as I could never guess how he would be the next day towards me: caring and loving or withdrawing and shutting down. But above all of this, I believed we loved each other and we were walking towards our future with both hearts full of dreams.

In July 2008, to celebrate one year dating and his birthday, we decided to travel to Tasmania where we enjoyed so much the cold weather and warming up together. We explored the famous Salamanca markets, Port Arthur Historic site and many other beautiful places around Hobart. Since my recovery from the ectopic pregnancy, we were trying to get pregnant again. He wished to be a father and ever since I was a little girl I knew I wanted to be a mummy, I was just waiting for the right man to marry and he was here already as my husband, so naturally we were already dreaming with it. Being a mum has been part of my deepest dreams for as long as I could remember in my life and because of my age and plus having just one side fallopian tube since the surgery, we wished not to wait too long to bring our baby to the earth. I got finally pregnant while we were in Hobart and of course realised weeks later after we returned. The day we returned from Tasmania, we went home to leave the suitcases and I took him to Maroubra beach as I had prepared a surprise birthday party for him with our closest friends. I organised all the details before departing to Tasmania with Bianca my friend. She and her husband organised everything for me to have a barbecue at the park, where we used to get together sometimes. His reaction was totally unexpected. When we arrived at the park I was already crying and was making all my effort to pretend I was happy. He got upset with me and was talking to me very rudely while driving instead of feeling happy for receiving an act of love, instead of feeling grateful and loving me for that, he actually hated me for it. I never understood that reaction of anger and I promised myself to never give him a birthday party again.

Soon after returning from Tasmania, we had a financial issue to solve about the excess of expenses being made on my credit card. It was the end of July and we were exchanging emails about payments pending from our travel to Tasmania. He asked to use my Brazilian credit card, which was linked with my savings account in Brazil. He said it was just for emergency and that he was going to pay it back before the due date arrived. The expenses were about $400 and included our hotel, car and ticket to Hobart. He also asked for the card days before for a job emergency to pay a van to do an airport pickup. In the emails, I was carefully writing to him and trying to assess the issue in a way that he will not feel upset and to avoid him shutting down. I was giving explanations and reminding him about our pre-agreement. His feedback was short and straight just ordering me to pay it myself with no excuses or explanations, no sorry, no open conversation and not having me accountable at all. I was feeling betrayed and thinking a lot about trust and his word of honour. I wrote to him asking him for us to create goal settings and financial plans short and long term, but that never happened. I was upset with the uncertain feelings, and unpredictable behaviour but was afraid to show it honestly when he arrived home because I was already trained by him that he wouldn't 'love me so much' if I wasn't happy with whatever he decided. We weren't talking much about important decisions, just small talk. Sometimes he was shutting down, and when that would happen, I was trying to reach him through writing letters to express my thoughts. I wasn't being heard and daring to start a dialogue would mean to him that I was making a big thing of nothing and he would blame me for creating a problem. I wasn't sure where I stood anymore.

The Good News

Weeks later I was feeling incredibly happy and feeling physically very different. I realised I was happily and blessedly pregnant. The day I realised I was pregnant was filled with joy and celebration inside my heart. I did the pharmacy test and it was positive! OMG! I wished to tell him immediately, but because of the last events that occurred, the energy was still cloudy between us and I was unsure about his reaction, and uncomfortable with his ups and downs of coldness towards me. I couldn't hold myself as I thought that the news would bring back his happiness so I sent him an email about the news while I was working on my assignments for my Hospitality Diploma. I was expecting him to arrive home over the moon, with flowers and hugging me and kissing. Instead, when he arrived, I felt surprised and disappointed with his distance. Although I think he was very happy, he was behaving very cautiously and not celebrating as much as I was expecting. He acted as if it were a normal day. He said, 'Take it easy, maybe it is not sure, we need to know for sure if all is okay, then we celebrate.' He could have been worrying about my health, or in fear of the future as the big boy responsibilities were now his reality, or something I will never know, but that wasn't the way to make his wife, a new mother, to feel loved at that time.

By this stage of our relationship, we still hadn't met each other's family, just had conversations by phone or Skype sometimes. I was always contacting my family with more frequency. He rarely used to contact his family, which for me was quite intriguing but each person has their own way to relate, so not a point to worry. Usually I was and I still am the one to give more attention to his family, talking nicely to everyone. He rarely was giving attention to my family and I was always puzzled that I had always to ask him to talk to my family when we received a call from Brazil. One of my goals in my relationship was seeing my husband being close to my father and my brother. But sadly that never happened, especially after my father and my stepmother came to visit us in Australia and then after the events that occurred in 2010–11.

My pregnancy was amazing! We were both so happy growing our family, he really wanted to be a daddy. I felt myself glowing, beautiful, shining, and healthy and with a kind of happiness in my soul that was unexplainable, which I described as a strong spiritual connection. Our family in Brazil were so happy too to be expecting their first grandchild, both in my family as in his. When I was about five months pregnant, we travelled to Brazil for the first time together, so we could be introduced to our families. We had exchanged emails to discuss the payment of the airlines tickets with my credit card. The thing is that the card limit required an earlier payment of the balance to achieve the amount we needed to spend with tickets, and he suggested that I would ask my father to pay a deposit for me to increase the limit and then 'I' would pay him back. Note that at this time, I wasn't working so many hours as before. My job role was events waitress and with pregnancy complications and tiredness I wasn't accepting heavy jobs. I wasn't feeling okay about him getting my father involved in it and putting me in a situation that I would ask him.

When we arrived in Brazil, we spent some time in Sao Paulo with his family and some time in Porto Alegre with my family. In Sao Paulo I felt very welcomed and cared for by his family. It was an interesting experience, as I could clearly see the unhealthy dynamics of the family and the individual issues of each of them, and how they related to each other. I had instantly deep compassionate feelings for his mother, for the way I saw she was being poorly treated. I could feel her pain through her eyes and the biggest red flag was waving in my face because I saw too much, more than what was being shown to me. Now I was already figuring out how all of that was influencing my husband's sub-conscious, bringing to our marriage the unhealthy pattern of his parent's relationship within the family. I left Sao Paulo profoundly puzzled, but after all, his father was treating me with so much respect and care and I respected it. I was also spoiled at his cousin's house for a special baby shower surprise to please me, which made me very happy. In Sao Paulo he was again paying some expenses with my Brazilian credit card, as he didn't have a credit card, including gifts for his family, which was worrying me a bit again. In Porto Alegre the card was also being used. In January 2009, I was again sending an email to him asking for the accountability with the fear feeling of his reaction because of past events.

My arrival in Porto Alegre, south of Brazil, was filled with joy mixed with emotional tears. My husband was greeted with so much affection by my family, especially my father, who was trying the best to make him feel at home. We had so many activities: my sister's wedding where I was going to be the maid of honour, my baby shower with a special barbecue at my parent's country house, visiting all the relatives, and medical appointments to make special pre-natal exams with the companion of my father, which was an emotional moment for me. I wished my mum could be there too, but we met another day, as she lives in another state. I also planned to take my husband to Gramado city to spend one weekend at the St. Humbertu's, the romantic hotel, for the biggest Christmas show called

'Natal Luz'. While in Porto Alegre, I was guided to a place where I had an unforgettable experience of receiving a special spiritual surgery in order to clean and heal my womb from undesired issues that were happening, saving my daughter and myself, which later was also confirmed and diagnosed by exams when returning to Australia.

Some Thoughts

The last seven years I have been forced by the life occurrences to use all the possible life skills learnt from my past experiences before coming to Australia. I was also forced to educate myself to new learning's through counselling, personal development courses, research, studies and books related to the relationship, family and people's behaviour and reactions. Life is a non-stop training process. It has been a period where I was exposed to a number of emotional hurt and traumatic challenges, dealing with numerous crisis situations where I decided to learn and grow, not just to survive but thrive. Writing and publishing a book about my unspoken story has been in my mind since 2011, when I faced one of the worst moments totally filled with fear and shadows, especially for my daughter. That was when my desire to publish a book began. From 2011 to now many different books were written in my mind until the moment I am now finalising this one. And I am still unsure about it. This book has a long story behind the book's story as I was having this strong desire to share the universal love and gratefulness I feel suppressed inside my heart, which was achieved while seeing the goodness around, combined with feelings of forgiveness towards the situation I lived, towards myself and towards to the one who put me through this; but also understanding why my sub-consciousness allowed this, giving permission for that to happen. I felt the call to turn my experience into something good for others and to be able to support and educate women who are experiencing similar situations, showing them that they have their beautiful and unique inner light, their light that they own inside ready to shine if believing in their worthiness and working in their inner peace, even when an unhealthy person is trying to break you, or the world is falling around you.

It is part of my belief that we can think about how we can prevent our negative past experience from impacting negatively our present or future, also how to improve our positive past experience to the level we will need now. One of the very important steps we need to take is to become aware of the childhood experiences that affected us the most, facing with reality and accepting with forgiveness. The next thing is to find out if we made a mistake while interpreting any of these events. For example, if your father was distant, you concluded that all men were cold, or if your mother didn't have a voice, you concluded that all women shouldn't have a voice. Those sub-conscious interpretations must be recognised as untruth so you will be able to reframe those patterns to your life. The third step for us in order to prevent this incorrect interpretation affecting our present is to replace that false belief with the right one that is true for you, not for anyone else. Getting to know a little of a partner's childhood and past experience will give you the tools to understand where they stand and why they behave in the ways that are sometimes out of control.

I really believe that no one wants to be in a situation of a broken family leaving broken hearts behind, distant from the family that was supposed to take responsibility and care of them. I refuse to believe that my former husband was aware of the emotional damage that was escalating between us, and how his distance was blocking all aspects of intimacy and silently and painfully slowly breaking us apart. How the lack of emotional intelligence and wise actions and refusing to humbly search for professional help, was transforming small issues into a disaster. I believe that everyone wants to do and to be better than the day before and that everyone can learn through mistakes to avoid repeating the same mistakes over and over again and getting the same bad frustrating results. I believe that everyone has the inner power to change what is not working and to open their mind to see what is really going on and bravely face it, accept it and take proactive action – if they really care about it. But people are different, and I have learnt through the years that we cannot have the same expectations and belief system that we have for ourselves to others. Somehow there are people that cannot find the way out, it's in their subconscious and it's something that if we do not accept and do not work on, it will never change.

What is very important to keep in mind is that understanding doesn't mean that we have to accept or agree with anything. Through knowledge we can learn to understand reasons or the cause of behaviour or emotional reactions, we can also have compassion and feel forgiveness, but accepting any kind of abusive behaviour in our families or society is something that we must not accept and we must break the cycle.

The impact the past has on your present is extremely powerful and unless you learn how to connect the dots from your past to your future then your whole life might be impacted in a way where the subconscious emotions will be driving you instead of being driven by your high and wise consciousness. We don't need to *be* what has happened to us. We are what we choose to become from that situation and that's why this book is called *Touched by Love – Turning Crisis into a Blessing*. I don't have any intention to hurt anyone through sharing my unspoken story. But I rose consciously to get to know that I have the power to give this experience, in the way I saw them, a meaning and an amazing purpose to serve people. The bad or good experience in our life does not have power over us, unless of course we let it. After all, our past just will continue to hurt if we insist to hold on to it. My life in Australia was profoundly touched by the love for my former husband, by the profound love for my daughter, by the love of connection with God, by the love of connection with community and by the love for life. I am here to let you know to pay attention and get awareness on what you experienced in your past, even in childhood, or as a teenager or in adulthood, you have the choice to find blessings and teaching from them or let yourself be dragged into the mud, destroying you instead of raising you. I did encounter blessings even when living the worst situation I could possibly live, I did encounter blessings in each person that was presented in my life when I most needed help and support to trespass the big challenges life was presenting.

A simple past event can greatly affect the person's present life. How many similar past events have contributed to your current beliefs? Can you imagine the hundreds of past events you've been through when you were a child that could have an effect on your system belief and in your life right now? From our childhood, our past life emotional experiences has influence on our present emotional reactions. The way we deal with emotions like rejection comes from unconscious thoughts and beliefs that we learn from childhood. That's why our childhood experiences and past memories are so important. Early childhood memories are the source from which children start to form their beliefs about the world. If for example a little child believes that his parents are giving more attention to his little sister, then he might develop the beliefs that his parents don't love him the way they love his little sister. But how can this past event affect the life of that child later on? Simply put, that child might always believe that someone else might be preferred over him wherever he goes. When that child grows up and gets married, he might start to believe that his wife is cheating on him whenever she smiles at other men. In such a case, the old belief that was developed in the past impacts the way the man sees life.

We are also the result of the limitations that were imposed on us. I believe I am a good product of the happenings in my life, but I can clearly see how much better I would be if I just knew earlier what life was really about and how past, present and future are connected. Our limited beliefs can impact our life without us being conscious and uncovering limited beliefs allow us to change and reach a life filled with joy. Choose your beliefs! Who is driving you? Our mind works on two levels: consciously when you are aware of your thoughts, and subconsciously when you aren't aware of the reason for your choice. Your action will be driven by deep memories, intuition, and belief system.

After reading this chapter, there are four actions that I would suggest:

1. Take an honest and balanced inventory of your life: memories of your childhood, your parents, your relationships and your emotional patterns. The personal cause, affect and damages. Your part in it and other people's part in it. Find the good and find the not so good. Analyse any patterns between events of your life. Avoid denial and face any triggers that will occur.

2. Assess yourself with clear and sober analysis. Find your core values: values from your past and values that are important to you now. Stick to it, and recognize if you are living with your values.

3. List your original personal goals and priorities and compare with what you are living now. Create new personal goals based on where you want to be and who you want to be.

4. Ask yourself, how can I use my past experience to serve people?

Chapter 2

Touched by Crisis

'Life always waits for some crisis to occur before revealing itself at its most brilliant.'

– Paulo Coelho

Crises will rise in our lives, no matter how we may try to avoid it. They are usually troubling, unwanted experiences or events that take us out of inner peace and our comfort zone. Typically crises result in some level of loss, but also can bring growth forcing change. In these moments it's easy to focus on all of the things that have gone wrong forgetting to see clearly and the opportunity ahead. In my understanding, crisis is the ultimate sign that something must be changed or improved. There is no growth without dealing with any level of crisis and getting us out of our comfort zone! People will always have the power to grow with their crisis experience, but if they don't learn much from that, it will be likely they will find themselves stuck in life, feeling victim and repeating patterns in the future. We must defeat crisis or crisis will defeat us.

It's always easier to focus on the loss and the heartbreak or the pain, but it's also important to remember all of those things that have gone right. It's important to remember all of the positive experiences and friendship and growth and laughter you have gained. Things you would have never taken part in, lessons you would have never learnt and people you would have never met if not facing crisis situations. Generally the most significant people in our lives sometimes are brought to our environment through crisis situations. And that has been happening to me the last five years.

Many times people naturally try to restore the order to their lives, as chaos and fear seems to show up. But if we learn to reframe how we view crisis, we might actually take advantage of it. There is a big potential in empowering people as human beings as the crisis unfolds into a game, as soon as we learn to stop resisting the unwanted change and start accepting and dealing with what is coming next.

I did achieve a profound personal change through the crisis situations I had encountered on my way, and all the situations had required loads of motivation, faith and intention to connect and believe on the power of the life transition. Any crisis situation we may face removes the safety boundaries that have given the sense of protection. It feels like a big storm turning our known life upside down changing everything we had, or thought we had. Normally we find ourselves trying desperately to return to the well known comfort zone, but the new situation will many times prevent that option when there is just one way to go: forward. And moving forward is where the opportunity is waiting for you!

But where we will find the opportunity? How can we see blessings in the middle of that dark and heavy storm? Where we can see the decisive point of a situation and how to do it? If we sincerely focus on the crucial cause of the situation, we may use awareness to honestly question ourselves where we going from here, what are the healthier choices I can make? What may be the consequences? In my personal learning, I tell you that crisis is very closely related with all the expectations that weren't met as we wanted.

Transformation is about to happen exactly on that point where we may feel there is no way to go, where you feel stuck and must urgently take decision. When I was facing my relationship issues escalating to 'marriage crisis' and soon turning into an abusive relationship and again escalating to a Domestic Violence category situation, I was feeling lost, I was feeling confused, I was feeling physically sick, because I didn't know what was really going on behind the events. I knew that something was seriously wrong, but I couldn't in reality put my finger on facts until I reached for help! I wanted desperately to know why, and more importantly how to fix my marriage, instead of giving up. But to fix a relationship takes two to walk in the same pathway of learning to heal and progress.

Later, in 2010, I found a book called *The Verbally Abusive Relationship* by Patricia Evans, which described in words exactly what I was experiencing. Reaching for information to educate myself about the events occurring in my relationship was the main kick-off action on starting to reach for support at the organisations in my neighbourhood. My gut feeling was clearly saying to me that I wasn't being treated fairly dealing with unkindly hot and cold behaviours, anger, disrespect, avarice, withholding, blaming, name calling and jokes, denial, and so many other categories of behaviour that was leading me to see my relationship and myself threatened. I knew I wasn't being treated with love and with respect, I knew that I was feeling sad and frustrated and feeling down, but I couldn't figure out why it was happening and I couldn't really be sure if he was realising how badly those events were damaging our family and himself.

So, crisis is simply the occurrence of a change being called, and if we don't listen or keep faking and pretending that it is not there, we will not be able to take responsibilities and take proper action focusing on growth and effective solution. If we release the need of control, we can engage and walk the road of change and often turn it into an amazing opportunity. But not releasing control and need of dominance will simply lead the crisis to a worst scenario, because when we don't face the fears of dealing with crisis with honest communication, we will let crisis defeat us. That is a killer for any relationship.

Crisis and relationship difficulties will tend to repeatedly continue until we realize that the pain of not taking action is bigger than the pain of the change. Relationship crisis has the opportunity to launch the couple into a new territory where growth may finally be achieved, or not. It is our decision as the pain of enduring through the challenges of crisis may actually enable this gain. I believe that relationship crisis can be a horrific experience, but it may also open the door to a more authentic examination of the relationship and many possibilities of a hopeful resolution. But it would occur just if both are willing to solve it with good heart, instead of the need of control, which leads to an escalated and irrational situation.

Things escalating

While living in Rockdale, our life was most of the time being filled with fun activities in between work and studies. Short travelling or exploring a new place and spending time with friends was our favourite activity. We loved to be together. We used to gather with friends at home for a meal or barbecue and any signs of distress, if occurred, were easily hidden. My marriage began filled with love and so much care, intimacy, friendship and openness and through the next year or two was quickly and silently being dragged to resentments and unsolved problems due to what appeared to me to be caused by miscommunication. It was hurting the way issues weren't taken seriously and I knew something different needed to be done soon, but life was busy now as a mother. I wasn't seeing him feeling strong and confident in some of the roles and responsibilities in the relationship as a husband. Being a father brought another role. I knew we loved each other so much, we had a sparkly physical attraction and sex was always intense, we were well known by our friends as a romantic couple and we wanted to be together. I was appreciating whatever he was doing as I really believed in my heart he was doing his best overall in his ability, with no intention to really target me or hurt me. I knew in my heart that his reactions or cold action towards me weren't matching his heart, it was something that was hurting him too and I wanted to stop the pain, fix what was threatening us to be happy as a family with the arrival of our princess, the seed of our love. That was what was in my heart and hopes.

By the time our much loved daughter was born, with 37.5 weeks pregnancy, I was already disappointed in my heart due to a number of small incidents and events that occurred in the last year. But I got incredibly busy with serious health issues and in love with my new challenge as a mother, I was filled with joy and contentment living the most important moment of my life and looking after myself so kindly as never before. During my pregnancy I was shining and feeling amazing! I was deeply grateful for receiving this gift from God. I was focused on the good and positive. And I was hoping that this moment would help to change things for better related to communication, sharing and respecting feelings and accountability. So, I really wanted to leave behind some of the events occurred even never hearing any "sorry". But, little 'put downs' and jokes that did really hurt are still in my mind until now. For example when I decided to educate myself reading motherhood books and doing research related to parenting and babies. No one in this world was born with parenting skills built in, and I wished we could learn together and share the entire amazing new world we were about to dive in. It hurt a lot when he refused to share this new adventure of learning with me, and on top of that saying to me that I was going to be a 'book mum'. That made me feel discounted and also alone on this beautiful journey of discovery. Trivializing and criticizing my effort on doing the right thing lead him on not learning anything and then I couldn't count on him for support, as he wasn't able to understand what I was talking about, but still behaving as knowing everything.

Day by day, as soon as something mean or unkind would happen, many other pleasurable moments would cover it up, making me feel again accepted and loved. It was like always dealing with rejection versus acceptation game, depending on my "good behaviour" or his moods. So it was like being "punished" with rejection or being "rewarded" with acceptation. The 'mismatched' situations were being left 'under the carpet', not being completely solved and we were pretending to be 'okay' the next day. I was getting uncomfortable with that game. I was just slowly finding it hard to be freely and totally me with authenticity as I was walking on shells to please him. I wanted to keep things peaceful, didn't want to be judged or criticized and I preferred to avoid any conflict. To avoid conflict and not being told that I was making a "big deal" or that I was the one "starting something" when trying to communicate to address issues, I slowly stopped sharing my feelings and needs to avoid rejection. Sometimes he was acting closed and distant and other times showing the need for affection and connection. I was observing and trying to figure out signs of answers to my questions. When issues or arguing occurred the conversation was turned around and the defensiveness and blaming was directed to me, making sure that everything was my fault.

For a long time I was trying to find where I was failing and get it right. I was giving all of me to our daughter's needs and to him, little was left for me. And to compensate I was mistakenly believing that if I treated him better, doing more things for him or being more 'lovable', the things would be better. Big mistake! I mean, showing love naturally would attract love, isn't it the universal law? But actually, it wasn't working and later I got to know why. Until things got seriously worst, I was still thinking that the events occurring were part of any beginning of relationships, emotional adjustments, getting to know each other in real life. But red flags about emotional immaturity were stuck in my mind, as for example when just months after our marriage, he was upset about one of our particular issues and surprisingly he mentioned divorce in the middle of the argument. I was shocked, as I wasn't sure if it was real or a threat. I thought to myself: 'My God, is our marriage based on such a fragile ground? Is this a joke?' For my values, that was unacceptable, as I knew that no marriage or family is built on such a fragile and weak base.

What I identified as an issue of poor communication was slightly escalating to controlling behaviour, disrespect and abuse, and what was strange to me is that the next day of any conflict, not a word was being said and the 'game' was to pretend nothing happened instead of having a healthy talk about the problems to clarify and improve. Again I found myself writing letters as I thought that if he was having blockages about expressing his feelings, and avoiding my feelings to be expressed, maybe a letter expressing how I was feeling about an issue would help him to 'listen' and understand without judgment and the need of being defensive, giving him space and a chance to think about it and then to come out expressing his opinion or needs in a considerate way, bringing back our connection and making our relationship stronger. In doing that, we could be proactive finding a solution to fix any issue that would be discretely rising and in need for change.

Pregnancy

My pregnancy was one of the most beautiful moments of my personal life as a woman. Being a mum was my deep desire from a young age, but of course I wanted it to happen at the right time with the "right" partner who would be able to fulfil the honoured place of husband and father. I wasn't sure anymore if I was really achieving that goal but was still living in hope that we would improve and grow through the issues we were facing. The level of pure love I felt while pregnant and still feel by now, is one of the most fulfilling feelings I could ever have experienced. Unfortunately, during my pregnancy, I had two big nasty uterine fibroids growing with our baby inside my womb. They were so big that by the time she was born, one was weighing one kilo and another weighing 700g. The worry was that earlier exams showed that one of them was pressing the baby's left side head. I was monitored weekly in the hospital. I was being very well cared for by the Royal Hospital for Women, and I was blessed to have an excellent and experienced obstetrician and gynaecologist closely looking after my case. Her name was Dr Swaran Nand.

Because of my age and uterine complications, Dr Nand decided for a caesarean section booked for 12 March. But while I was having routine exams on 9 March, she decided to arrange my admission on that very day, not leaving the hospital anymore, and having the caesarean section booked as emergency class 4 for the next morning! We both were very excited but also a little scared.

Joahnne was born on 10 March 2009, at 14:20h and the delicate and emergency caesarean section class 4 was considered successful. Although she was diagnosed with a heart murmur and cerebral cyst, she was healthy and incredibly beautiful. I was being carefully treated because of the uterine fibroids that couldn't be touched or removed during caesarean and continued living inside my womb after the birth. I was alone with no family around but I had girlfriends who were coming up to visit and support me somehow. Joahnne and I were discharged on 16 March to go home. At home I wasn't feeling well physically, I knew something wasn't right. With a newborn baby, feeling sick and coping with all the household chores and loss of sleep and loss of eating, and still trying to keep myself okay for my husband when we arrived home, I was missing my family being close to me.

Challenge about health

About four week's post-partum, the uterine fibroids decided to leave my body while on the toilet. What a nightmare! While in that appalling situation, and with Joahnne crying, I was stuck and scared on the toilet and calling him to come home quickly. He became nervous to handle the situation, as I needed, which was life threatening. Instead of him driving me to my hospital, to my doctor, where Joahnne and I was going to feel safe and well cared, he drove me instead to the closest hospital from home. That was the most horrible and fearful situation I ever had in my life. When I realised I was in front of the wrong hospital, I refused to get out of the car. 'I've asked and begged to be taken to The Royal Hospital as they would know exactly and quickly what to do with me.' He yelled back to me screaming to get out of the car right now! I tried to say that I didn't have a good feeling about this. It didn't matter about my appeal.

So, my feelings were right. There I was, in an emergency room, with a newborn baby exposed, waiting long hours through the night while the doctors were trying to communicate with The Royal Hospital to figure out my situation. I again asked three times to be transferred but clearly I wasn't being heard. As a result, I spent the night there alone and Joahnne with the nurses in another room and the worst was that I got the unpleasant consequence: body infection.

The next morning, 7 April, I was finally transferred from St George to The Royal with prolapsed infected fibroid and carrying my lovely Joahnne that was always with me. The fibroid was surgically removed on the same morning but the infection didn't go away. For 25 days Joahnne and I were hospitalised. I was having high fevers every day, needles around my arms connected with a machine, strong chemicals being injected into my body, doctors coming in and out every hour expecting that my fevers would go away so they could decide to book another surgery or not. I was fighting for my life and the biggest thing that helped me was holding on to my faith! With all that happening, I was trying to cope with so much love and commitment as a new mother, day and night. At that time I was so busy with my baby needs that actually I wasn't fully aware of the serious situation I was experiencing. I put all my strength together, resilience, happiness, and also kindness with everyone in the hospital. The love for my daughter and determination to stay with her made me stronger. I made it through because of my faith in God and in the angels that were looking after us. I was praying every night to have my body cleaned and be given the blessed opportunity to raise my daughter, as she needed me so much. At the end of April the good news arrived and we went back home! I was feeling so blessed and grateful for that!

Ironically, the very first afternoon we returned home, the second fibroid decided to give me a hard time as well and I had to return urgently to the hospital that same night where I had another surgery and stayed more days to recover. All the team doctors that were involved with my case, used to tell me to write a book about it, that I was one rare case and that they didn't remember about having a patient like me, having the body self-expelling the fibroids and self-cleaning itself. So, of course, I remembered about the spiritual surgery I mentioned in chapter 1, when visiting my family in Brazil, and now I was aware of the profound importance of that event.

The beginning of motherhood was filled with joy and happiness but also was pretty hard while slowly recovering physically and emotionally, experiencing poor sleep, living in auto-mode, tiredness, excess of household, but coping – or thinking I was coping. I was still in strong pain and recovering and under strong medications when Joahnne was three months old and had her turn to have a surgery. Joahnne suffered from constipation since birth and had developed hernias in her tiny abdomen from forcing to go. Oh God, that was even harder than my medical challenges: I was alone in the hospital, handing her over to the doctors for surgery and then waiting the longest time in my life while sitting and praying in the waiting room. But my worst feeling happened when just after her surgery, I anxiously went to pick her up from the lovely nurses and I saw her tiny little arms covered with big needles. I couldn't cope with that because I was still healing from the painful feelings of having my arms daily pierced in the hospital to look for veins to receive medicines. When I saw her I needed a moment to recover before putting back my motherhood strength to do my job. One day, I got so exhausted that I fainted on the floor of the bathroom, when quickly trying to stand up to attend my baby. I was pushing myself through to the limit.

I am sharing a tiny piece of that traumatic experience because that has been a very significant and powerful episode in my life. In the moment of crisis, we can build bridges if we choose to be wise, but if not the abyss will prevail.

Back Home

After all of that, there I was back home trying to move life forward, being incredibly busy at home, exhausted many times with the job but also living the most blessed days in my life as a mother, and everyday being thankful for the opportunity to be alive.

Joahnne was almost three months old now. We were both recovering from our surgeries. I barely could move or sit properly even to feed her but was doing everything. I believed I was doing my best as a mother, wife and also housekeeper, trying to cover all the needs required. Giving much more from me than receiving and feeling already emotionally and physically exhausted.

One morning my husband became very upset and angry about things that I couldn't even understand or remember, and he left the house yelling at me that I should come back to work right now and left roughly slamming the door behind him. I remember I was about to feed Joahnne at that time. She got frightened and started to cry because of the door noise. I started sobbing, feeling unprotected in the middle of my emotional and physical exhaustion of having no sleep for many nights in a row. I was the only one to attend Joahnne day and night, so he would have his sleep and be rested for his hard work the next day. He said one day he knew everything about babies already. I was now a mum, a protective mum and I was now standing for what I learnt and believed from my core and heart, to be the best for Joahnne and trying not to feel controlled by him.

Because of Joahnne, I wished to move to an area more appropriate to raise a child. At the beginning, he wasn't very happy with the idea, but again my faith helped me to make things happen. He received a job offer in Northern Beaches. It wasn't really his 'thing', but he was excited with that and off we went to make house inspections during the weekends with a three-month-old baby.

When Joahnne was four months old, we finally moved from Rockdale to live in Northern Beaches, Dee Why Beach. I never liked living in Rockdale, so I was over the moon to live in such a beautiful area, especially because my father and my stepmother were already planning to visit us for the first time to get to know their beloved grandchild.

When Joahnne was one year old my parents travelled from Brazil to Australia for the first time. They came with so much good intention to enjoy this moment and also supporting us emotionally and financially. I was so excited and happy that they were here and so proud to receive my parents in my home for the first time as a married woman. Unfortunately, by the time my parents arrived, my relationship was broken. I couldn't cope with his reactions anymore and I was being reactive as well, feeling protected by my father. The controlling behaviour was escalating fast and I remember finding myself in many tricky situations, as nothing that I was doing was enough.

The ego was dominating and the harsh words or the silence were his two big weapons, and that was killing me inside. I was starting to have shorter patience but was still hoping that it was going to stop as soon as our defences were downloaded to give space to what was really important, realising that that silent battle was not going to take us anywhere and that I wasn't his enemy. I didn't know what to expect from him anymore, I was dealing with a complete stranger. Many times he was making me feel guilty for his behaviour, as if I was the reason for his actions so the consequence was 'punishing' me with something that would emotionally hurt. I was refusing to believe that this was consciously or intentionally happening, because my heart couldn't accept that hate would possibly have the power to cover love. I wanted to help us to go through it but I knew that it required two of us, and it wouldn't be possible with just one. Funny enough, based on his emails, he was seeing everything opposite, as I was his mirror.

While my family was here, we had good times but also times of distress and unnecessary conflict to the point that my father tried to talk to him using his wisdom and own life experience with my mum to help to clear his vision. But being the guy who believes he knows everything and no one needs to tell him what he should or should not do, the conversation had little or no effect. My father brought presents for us and a special one for him; a Brazilian barbecue inside his luggage. I was so grateful, but I remember feeling uncomfortable or embarrassed by my husband's cold approach towards them.

Even though my father was feeling sad about his daughter being treated badly by her husband, he wanted to help him financially to apply for our Australian residence. My family witnessed how he was treating me and got not just sad and worried, but upset with him. They were almost deciding to return earlier back to Brazil. My stepmother has a very strong personality and she was angry about what she witnessed. I was deeply ashamed and disappointed as that wasn't what I really wanted to show them. I was imagining how much I would make everything go right, if his family was here instead.

My parents left Australia very disappointed with his behaviour and worried about Joahnne and me. At the airport, I said to my dad: 'Dad, I can't cope with what's happening anymore but I really will do anything possible to keep my family together because there is love under all of those issues. I believed that whatever was happening inside him, it would shift if we could unblock the real reason. But if it continued like that, I wasn't sure if I would still be married in one year from here.'

Little did I know that over the next year that things were going to be worse. It was all very unpredictable as there were again periods of peaceful days. But those days slowly got much rarer. He was drinking much more than before, not just on weekends, staying at barbecues on the beach with his mates or our group of friends until night time, going out and coming home late at night and many times I was seeing him drunk when arriving and just lying down on the couch to sleep until morning. That definitely wasn't the role model I wanted my daughter to learn from her father. When his mates were calling him to make barbecues, even if we planned something with Joahnne, he would leave us at the pool or wherever and run to the supermarket and bottle shop to meet his mates. I couldn't count or trust on him. I was many times completely ignored, receiving sarcasm, hostility, silence, and recently some name-calling. I never heard one sorry and in exactly one year after my father visited, the situation got to the extreme ending to a 'forced' physical separation.

Just before Joahnne was turning two years old, he was clearly in war mode and I was already in so much fear. By this time I was getting sick and throwing up in the mornings, unable to eat I lost almost 10kg, emotionally drained, feeling lost, hopeless, very confused, rejected, and frustrated. I started to desperately reach for help. The emotional and verbal abuse was starting to escalate to the physical; one day I got myself to the hospital because he pushed our daughter's highchair on top of my foot, another day he was so angry that he pushed me against the wall with his hands on my neck, the worst was seeing his eyes filled with hate. The financial control was in place for a long time already and it was getting worse. The only thing still keeping me on my feet was the deep love for my daughter, and for her I would be able to do anything. Many of my girlfriends were meeting me at the playground with our children and seeing me in such a desperate situation.

For Joahnne's second birthday party, I planned a party at the park with her friends and our friends, on the grass in front of the playground. He decided to leave us by ourselves, not to help with anything and disappeared all day. Just three days before her party, he had announced he wasn't going to pay for anything. I found myself alone with her but I wouldn't give up on her party because of him and I made this happy party happen with the last minute help of all my girlfriends. I did my best to give the best day for my daughter even without his support, without his presence, without his money, without whatever. That day was the end of my patience and I decided that I must leave that toxic relationship, but yet was still feeling sorry for him and for us as a family. There is nothing to gain and too much to lose with stubborn and arrogance.

At that point I was already receiving orientation and education. I went to countless community centres; I went to the domestic violence organisation. I went to the police station. I was willing to get to know what possibly would happen if that threatening situation continued and what options were available, before deciding to leave. With so much new knowledge through reading, seminars and talks with social workers, I could finally gather enough strength to accept the road ahead to be taken.

Still no matter how painful was the path between the feelings of the desire to love him and look after him after all I experienced, or running away from him to stop the hurt, I believe that that happened because of the different meaning/view existing behind the events or behind each person's perception. I believe that the story we have with people is the story we're supposed to have with them for veiled reasons. We are here in this life to grow and our growth is possible only through connections, connection with people and earth. There is no good or bad experience, only experiences where you grow from one point to another. Crisis is the way to grow and see where you are stuck in your life otherwise it will keep you frozen, so make the most of the crisis and you can win! Every experience in life brings you the opportunity to be one step forward in your self-development.

When we are out of our comfort zone we are forcibly pushed to find a way to solve our challenges, and that leads to growth and higher level of change, if not caught in self-defence. Maybe we might be blind to see any blessings on the road of crisis, but if we have a deep look in our past, we will see how much we have grown and how much we have been blessed and learnt through our crisis situation.

Self-defence is a big block that leads to denial (conscious or subconscious refusal to face the truth) and fantasy (avoiding real world, emotional isolation, withdrawal to avoid rejection, aggression, reverting back to a less threatening time, taking out frustration on others, projection, blaming others, making excuses for poor behaviour). If we have a look at the above elements of self-defence, we can actually open ourselves to more learning situations and start to see the blessings through our crisis and how to benefit with all the situations that the crisis is going to be able to give us.

Believe you won't be confronted with crises you can't handle. When we are confronted with what appears to be a crisis, the deeper you look, the easier it will see it. When you see it, you can say goodbye to its corresponding frustration, depression and anger. Trees stand strong because of the wind; no person can be strong without a challenge. Be thankful for yours. Any time we withdraw from something that is challenging, that may be the very thing that we need to grow through. Instead of running from challenge, be wise on tackling it and take advantage of an opportunity to make a difference and serve. Many people have the greener pasture syndrome, but everywhere there is pain and pleasure, and that is life. Face your challenges, find your blessings and, growth from there and change your world to what you really want. If there is someone important in your life that isn't getting it, it is not your fault; it's their own journey of growth. Some people have the ability to learn through love, others through pain.

When you find yourself in front of two paths to choose from and afraid to choose both, that will keep you frozen. I was in front of my two paths – stay or go – waiting for a sign to decide one of the paths for me. I wanted the best for my daughter and the best could be both of the paths, depending on our decisions, actions and choices. The decision must to be taken! The challenge with relationships is that it doesn't matter how much effort you put in; if the other party is blind, the 'boat' will sink. And when we can feel the boat sinking, there are two choices to choose from: sink together or jump out of this boat and swim to a better and safer place. I still feel that I was the one physically leaving the relationship, but I did that because emotionally I was being left while within the relationship. As a metaphor, I felt like I didn't jumped from the sinking boat, but I was pushed off it on the rough stormy ocean carrying our daughter on my back, struggling but making sure I will not drown while swimming to the nearest island. The island for me was the Women's Refuge. Life was still about to unravel for me that the relationship crisis I was facing and dealing with an abusive relationship was going to look small after leaving, as you will read in Chapter 6, Touched by Decision. The big crisis and challenge I was going to face during the next months was going to be tremendously bigger. Because when we are practically taken from our home by the police to go to a women's refuge with our children to be protected, grabbing what we can to make children's life better, we don't realise how much is taken to organise the big mess. Plus, while trying to organise the big mess, we still will probably have to cope with all kinds of threats and manipulation from our ex-partner, as the anger and revenge will be greater after we leave. Imagine how much time is taken up by leaving Domestic Violence, plus emotional stress under surviving mode. The list is huge: housing issues (facing the risk of homelessness); court and lawyers; isolation; mental health and healing through counselling and other options; protecting children emotionally and addressing their issues; financial challenges; child support; countless appointments with school, childcare, social worker, bank, work, immigration and much more; paperwork, applications, Centrelink, legal aid, planning future about study and work, loosing or keeping your job, and much more above all the day-by-day responsibilities that we have already as a mother covering our children's needs. Facing the big threat of not having permission to leave the country with your children or worse be forced to leave the country without your children.

Crisis really touched me, but I never had a thought to give up, because I had a big why: my daughter.

If you are feeling challenged by any crisis situation in your life, try to focus on the result and outcomes for whatever you want to achieve. Focusing specifically on the result you want to achieve will ensure that crisis creates the blessings and opportunities in your life, taking you to a positive turnaround.

F – Faith in what you want to achieve will keep your vision inspired only on the positives of the purpose you wish to reach.

O – Out coming results based on your attitude and ability to visualize your expectation.

C – Connections through effective and pro-active communications is the key of change process. Get connected being kind and honest. Don't be afraid to share your story.

U – Uniform, be uniform by being constant, stable and consistency on your decisions

S – Safe, whatever you do, do it in a safe way.

Chapter 3

Touched by Awareness

'Let us not look back in anger, nor forward in fear, but around in awareness.'

– Unknown

What is really awareness anyway?

We experience who we are through our awareness of what is going on around us, our perceptions, our thoughts, our senses and the emotions that we experience everyday. This is what makes us who we are, it is our awareness that makes us human, and it is how we navigate our lives through events and crisis situations. We must remember that our true essence is our true soul and spirit. It is not the result of what we do, or say or think or feel, which helps us to understand our experience of life, but they are not who we really are.

Understanding this, being aware of self, means that you can see problems for what they really are, not how we would prefer to see them. When we stay aware we can adjust how we relate to others and deal with situations more positively. Sometimes this hurts, because we may need to face the truth of a situation, or a truth about ourselves. When we are aware we can be more objective, and then we can be kinder on ourselves.

It was only when I read Daniel Goldman's book, *Emotional Intelligence* that I really started to understand how it all works. I understood that emotional intelligence was divided into two categories, each with two elements. The first category is Personal Competence, which includes self-awareness, when you are aware of yourself through your thoughts and feelings, and self-management, when you are managing your behaviours through choosing your actions. The second category is Social Competence, which includes social awareness, when you have empathy towards others through putting yourself in their place, and, relationship management, which is how you create and maintain relationships with others.

I needed this, because things weren't going better in my marriage, communication was totally blocked and accusations, blaming, judging, and denial were clearly present. I was really getting fed up by having to walk on eggshells every day and trying to 'be nice' to someone who was hurting me so much, putting me down and getting worse daily. I was always primarily using my energy for providing Joahnne's needs, all her needs, and then trying to maintain my sanity and peace of mind in the middle of so many things to do, people to talk to, information to receive and future decisions that were going to be required.

I realised that being aware didn't necessarily mean that I understood what was happening and why it was happening. I am an empath, which means that I take on the feeling of others. So it was even more difficult for me to understand what was happening, because when he had a bad day, I had to try even harder to preserve myself and make a very happy day for our daughter. My first emotional reactions were always trying to understand his feelings and find out a reason for the poor choices and a solution. Little did I know that when dealing with a narcissist type of person, this is not achievable.

Later I understood that a narcissist will only focus on himself or herself, even when it hurts the people that they love. The thought of being vulnerable is terrifying to them, and this leads to the development of a false self. Guarding their own emotional wounds at all costs, they are not capable of having authentic and intimate relationships, leading to deep unresolved hurt and conflict between narcissists and people that love them. Plus, they will always think they are above everyone, should never apologize unable to see the real self they are showing.

I was also feeling frustrated and angry about not being loved as I thought I deserved to be. I'm a very empathetic person and I also had compassion for him and love. I was feeling sorry that he was acting cruel against me and wondering what I could do to help him face reality and change his behaviour realising how much he was breaking my heart and our hopes. Even when being touched by awareness, I was still feeling a victim of the situation. Very soon the word 'victim' changed completely in my vocabulary replacing it with the word of 'survivor'.

The real awareness about my relationship started to happen at the end of 2009. I was touched by awareness through reaching a number of services available and was informed that, based on all of the evidence and events I was reporting, the social workers and community services explained that my relationship was escalating to a dangerous situation, that Joahnne and I were exposed, and that I had to face it and make a decision before worse things happened. I wasn't just experiencing a normal marriage conflict or lack of communication in our relationship but something called an abusive relationship, which is classified as domestic or family violence in Australia. I was shocked! I started connecting the dots and realised that the issue was bigger than I had imagined, shocked with the high statistics and number of women living similar or much worst situations, surprised with the excellent service available to support women and children to receive what was needed to go through with such a delicate situation.

People want different things from a relationship. Some want to be loved, some want a sexual relationship, some want romance and others want someone to be close to. It takes time to find someone who wants the same as you. When I was feeling sad and hurt, I was asking myself, is this real love? Is love supposed to hurt? Does he know or see what is happening? What is his perception about it all?

I was finding myself trying to see the situation through his eyes to be able to help him. I thought our relationship was fantastic at first, and I knew all about the bright side of his personality too, so I needed to understand why he was acting with hate towards me? Where was the cause of the reactions?

A healthy relationship is based on respect, so we could have a look at the respect checklist. Someone who respects you will treat you fairly and accept you for who you are, not for what you do or do not do. If someone is treating you with respect you will:

1. Feel free to go at your own pace in the relationship.

2. You will feel good about yourself.

3. Free to say no to things you don't want to.

4. Safe and never scared.

5. Free to see other friends and family when you want.

6. Free to change your mind.

7. Supported to make your own decisions.

8. Free to express your opinions and beliefs.

9. Free to end the relationship if that's what you want.

I encourage you to have a look at the above aspects and see if you feel like that. If you relate to those aspects, yes, you are being treated fairly and with respect and you are in a healthy relationship. Because being in a healthy relationship is when you have fun together. You're both able to be yourself, not just a friendship, but also a physical relationship. You can have differing opinions and interests without being pressured to change your mind. You will feel supported to achieve your personal goals. You will actively listen to each other; you will compromise, say sorry and talk arguments out. You don't have to spend all your time together. You can spend time alone, or with friends, or with family and feel safe and happy.

You will both feel complete individuals, bringing to the relationship the best that you have in your personality. You will feel free but will compromise and freedom is the power or a right to act, speak or think as one wants, the state of not facing imprisonment or slavery.

Most importantly, both are open to learn, both are open to grow and both are open to develop their skills in a relationship to turn themselves into better people in the future.

Change is part of growth. Change is part of a relationship. If someone says to you, 'Oh, you can't change me, I don't want to change, this is how I am', this person is actually not open for growth, not open for change and he will be stuck in his miserable life, bringing problems and getting consequences for those problems created.

I was willing to know what was going on with my relationship and what was going on with me, I wanted to understand him. I wanted desperately to find a solution to surpass the real cause giving us difficulty and learn from the experience making our relationship stronger for future conflicts. I tried to invite him to couple counselling which would help us to open ourselves and heal our problems to be happy as a family providing the life our beautiful and innocent daughter deserves.

I was reaching out to community services, I was reaching out to counsellors, I was reaching out to social workers, I was reading books, I was trying to reach for knowledge to be able to understand and change too. I believed that the behaviour was from sub-consciousness and if he wasn't able to see it, he wouldn't be able to take better decisions. But it was a must to have him bravely on board, instead of hiding his head in the sand like an ostrich when scared.

I didn't want to give up on us, I wanted to keep our family together and stay on his side to help him to emerge from the emotional issues and was desperately trying to change our relationship but it wasn't possible as I was destroying myself in this process and even worst it was really affecting my emotional ability to be the best mother possible as I was stuck in a trap trying to protect myself and the effect on our daughter.

If you are trying to save a relationship, you are probably taking some of these approaches as I did:

- analysing your spouse to no end
- talking about your problems with friends or family
- trying all sorts of communication skills designed to improve relationships
- talking to other couples to see what they have done
- reading self-help books about relationships, and maybe even attending workshops.

It is a common thing to do if we are looking for answers and for the missing key that will finally reveal what we needed to do. But all of that doesn't work when you are dealing with an abusive relationship, and that was where I was. The approach must be very different. If you recognise that you aren't in an abusive relationship, but just experiencing temporary marital crisis, here some solutions on how to improve your relationship:

1. Ask yourself how you would like the relationship to be different.

2. Set aside a time to talk to each other about your relationship and how you are feeling or thinking.

3. Listen to each other and try to understand the other person's feelings.

4. Say what you want and be prepared to negotiate.

5. Try to find things you both like to do together. Don't just do what the other person likes all the time.

6. Allow each other time to do your own thing, to be alone or to be with other friends or family.

When you are in an abusive relationship, the steps above will not likely happen because the controlling person has no desire for mutuality and the possibility for a happier relationship only exists if both parties are willing to change.

I don't believe that any man or any person wants to see themselves as an abuser, bully or an unhealthy person in a relationship. I believe that it's not on purpose, because I believe in the best of each person in the world. Everyone is trying to do their best, but that is my belief system. People are different and sometimes they don't recognise the same things. What happens is that people live in different realities. An abuser lives in a totally different reality and I will speak a bit more about different realities in the next chapter.

When someone who supposedly loves you treats you badly, it can be very hurtful and devastating. They might not always treat you like this, they might sometimes be hot and cold, be really nice and loving, so you might think it's not that bad or this is just how it is, or he is just having a bad day, but you should always be treated with respect.

Here are some warning signs that your relationship may be abusive even if you're not experiencing all of that yet. Any one of these warning signs is enough to indicate that this could turn into or is even already an abusive relationship. It sometimes starts with a subtle sign and then escalates and grows bigger:

- If your partner controls you, wants to know your every move and checks up on you. Won't allow you to make your own decisions, what to wear or eat, where to go, how to spend your money, or he stops you having your own money especially if you're not working and looking after the kids, if he starts to cut out the credit card or leaving without any money with the kids. The other aspect is controlling your life through jealousy.

- He is always suspicious of you. He can't actually trust in himself, that's why they don't trust anyone else. You'll find you are always watching what you say or do in case it upsets them. Often accusing you of flirting when you aren't. Isolates you, cuts you off from everyone or stops you from seeing family or friends and this could be very subtle. He wouldn't say that but he would make situations where you feel bad if you want to meet with your girlfriends or you're speaking with your family.

- Lacks respect, puts you down, calls you names, criticises you a lot, speaks badly about you or other women, puts women down and thinks men are better than women. I remember I was being called pig, dull, stupid and some other names that were very hurtful. That stays in my heart even today. Up till today, when I hear the word 'pig' anywhere, even for a joke, it hurts me.

- They can often be angry. Angers easily, yells and shouts, complains a lot about other people makes harsh judgements about others, becomes really annoyed with anyone whose view is different. Blames everything on other people. Doesn't apologise or admit mistakes.

- They pressure you or force you to do things that you don't feel comfortable with. That may include sex. I believe that sex must just occur when you are spiritually connected with someone and you feel loved and respected by them. That's when you can give your body. I am a person who's not able to give my body to anyone who wouldn't conquer my soul first through the eyes. The soul must be connected because in spirituality you need to be very careful about giving your body to someone to play with if you're not in a very deep soul connection. Because sex can affect your energy very badly.

- They rush the relationship. Push you to become more involved or serious more quickly than you'd like.

Abuse happens when one person tries to control or hurt another person. Abuse includes:

- Emotional put downs, and name-calling.

- Emotional or physical threats to hurt you.

- Sexually touching, forcing, or tricking you to do something that you don't want to do.

- Financially controlling your money or how you spend it.

- Socially controlling your contact with friends or family.

A healthy love relationship is when two people who are whole and complete have happiness within themselves. Standing upright, not leaning on or tangled up with the other person. They are able to live their own lives. They have an abundance of love to share with the other person. They choose to stay together, because they are free to be individuals who are sharing their lives together. They can come close together and choose this position temporarily; they can walk hand in hand as they might do in parenting and they can even move apart and have their own careers, their own lives and their own friends. Their choice to stay together is out of love for each other rather than needing to stay together because of some unmet emotional needs. A healthy love relationship gives both people the space to grow and become themselves.

The power and control diagram is a particularly helpful tool in understanding the overall pattern of abusive and violent behaviours, which are used by the abuser to establish and maintain control over his partner. Very often one or more violent incidents are accompanied by an array of these other types of abuse. They are less easily identified, yet formally establish a form of intimidation and control in the relationship.

An abusive partner can have a charming side too. Sometimes he seems to have two personalities. His behaviour can change drastically from one moment to the next. This is not insanity, it is manipulation. The games and abuse an abusive partner plays with your emotions can make you feel crazy, inadequate, guilty or confused. It is often hard to pin down emotional abuse and your partner may say he behaves as he does because he loves you. Emotional abuse is as real as physical abuse. They are similar in almost every way, except that physical bashings and bruises are visible, while emotional ones are not. Someone experiencing emotional abuse can feel just as fearful or trapped as someone experiencing physical abuse.

What effect does emotional abuse have? When a woman is experiencing emotional abuse, she may be affected in many different ways. She may experience panic, despair and feel that there is no way out. She may feel worthless or unattractive and lose or gain weight. Or she may become dependent on alcohol or other drugs.

Sometimes a woman may not realise that what she's feeling is caused by the abuse. Women want to be responsible for the emotional wellbeing of their partners and families. Sometimes this is at a cost to them.

How do you tell if your relationship is emotional abuse? Here are some definitions to get out of confusion about definitions:

Domestic Violence refers to acts of violence that happen in domestic settings who have/had an intimate relationship, including emotional, psychological, financial, sexual and physical.

Emotional/Psychological violence can include a range of controlling behaviours including financial control, isolation from friends/family, humiliation, threats with injury or death and threats against children.

Family Violence is a broader term than domestic violence referring to violence between any family members. Anything leading to a family member to feel fearful or controlled, including youth against parents or elder abuse.

Intimate Partner Violence is the most common form of abuse against women and stands for any behaviour within an intimate relationship causing harm to those involved.

Non-partner sexual assault stands for a sexual violence perpetrated by strangers, acquaintances, peers/friends, teachers, and family members.

Does your partner show jealousy or possessiveness, always keeping track of you? Accusing you? Calling you names? Destroy your sentimental items or personal property? Threaten to hurt you or your children or stop you seeing your children if you leave? That's the big one. Make all the important decisions or undermine your decisions. Tell you all the problems are your fault. They promise to change and charm. Gifts or affection if you say you want to leave the relationship. They act nice and sweet and suddenly become angry or violent. Put you down in front of other people or in private situations?

What can you do to escape from emotional abuse? If you find some of the behaviours your partner is using are abusive, your next step is to look for professional help to make a plan to survive. You begin moving forward once you stop looking for the magic button that will change your partner or save the relationship. That's what works. You can't change anyone and you can't heal a relationship by yourself because it takes two to have a relationship.

Once you do this, you are on the path, which will save you and perhaps your children. Leaving an emotionally abusive relationship is not easy. Remembering these important points may help you take this step. Abuse is a game of power and control, it is not love.

Trust your instincts, if the relationship is not good for you, plan to get out. Know that you cannot work it out in an abusive relationship. Know that you can't save your partner at the expense of your own life, sanity or happiness. Don't feel sorry for who is abusing you, no more excuses, no more lies. Get help for you, not your partner, believe in yourself and focus on you and your children's needs. Gather support for yourself. Tell people the truth about what is happening and consider joining a women's group.

Take one step at a time, even if you're angry, hurt and disappointed. It is normal to grieve, keeping a diary or journal of events and writing about your feelings may help. Remind yourself that what you know is real.

We can't let people scare us; we can't go our whole lives trying to please everyone else. We can't go through life worried about what everyone else is going to think. Whether our hair, clothes, what we have to say, how we feel, what we believe and what we want, we can't let the fear of their judgement stop us from going for it, because if we do, we are no longer ourselves. We are someone everyone else thinks we should be. When reaching awareness, true freedom is available and freedom would embrace us, beckoning us to be still.

Stop the distractions, cease the endless activities and become aware of the moment. Be present. All answers, all realisations are here right now. Believe that. You need to believe in yourself and believe in a higher power in the universe. Whatever you call that; I call it God, but my faith saved me many times in all my crisis situations. Have you been drifting off into your mind into stories of your life's drama? Have you lost your sense of self in endless activity? Are you doing almost anything to distract yourself to avoid feeling?

Please, wake up to all distractions, all of them. Just breathe and fully welcome whatever you are feeling at this moment, even if it's only a whisper, just feel what's here, be fully present to it, dive into it. Here are your three keys to liberation: acceptance, action and gratitude.

Chapter 4

Touched by Reality

'*Accept what is, let go of what was, and have faith in what will be.*'

– Sonia Ricotti

Facing reality is one of the more courageous acts that you can have in your life. When you decide to face reality you show yourself that you're open to accept what's really going on in your life and what's really happening behind the scenes. When you accept what's really going on you're ready to learn and to take action to change, grow and to be grateful.

Since the beginning of the crisis in my relationship, when my heart and my soul was being broken, I knew a long time before that something was wrong, I just didn't know what and was ignoring the signs. Also I didn't have the knowledge. Facing reality gave me a name for what I've suffered. When you name the feelings, when you name what's going on it's easier for you to recognise and stop denying and face your reality to be able to take action to change your situation.

One of my biggest questions to myself was, *what's wrong with people who are verbally abusive or emotionally abusive?* I was always asking myself why he was so nice one day and so mean the next, where was the kind person that I married and why months later he started to show a different man that I couldn't recognise? I always wanted to see the best thing in people. I believe people can change, but we cannot control other people's behaviour, we can just control ourselves. We need to rely on the hope that that person really wants to see what's going on with them and find solutions for the issues being caused.

Another question I was thinking sometimes, *what would it take for a verbally abusive person to change?* Can any abusive man stop their abusive behaviour at some point? I believe any person can change and I believe that they can best make these efforts if they really desire from deep within their heart, if they are grounded in the knowledge and if they're hoping to learn and receive the acknowledgement about the reason for their behaviour. Then they can see what's going on, accept that, stop the denial and start to take action. Change is possible when the pain is higher than the resistance of change.

Sometimes I was hearing, 'Oh, you are trying to start a fight.' So he had a motive behind his behaviour. Or, 'You just want to be right.' Or 'You don't feel that way.' So he was choosing my feelings or telling me that I was too sensitive. Abusers make these statements as if they are Gods, as if they live with their partner in soul and mind and know these things for truth. When I was trying to make a point and talk about the issues raised, it was like, 'What's wrong with you? Are you making a big thing out of nothing?' It was the attitude and many other forms of denial.

While he was brushing issues and problems under the carpet, more unsolved problems were rising and growing and building up one on top of another. Sometimes he would say to me that my feelings were wrong and my perceptions of reality were wrong, but actually, it's because he wanted to control my feelings and choices. If both people face the reality and stop the denial and have the humility to find help, I believe that there is a possibility for a happy relationship.

In order to fix or determine if you can have a happy relationship with your partner, you need to find a way to respond in a specific way, a way that will request change.

You can have two fears: the fear of loss of love or the fear of loss of self. But fear must not stop you from what is important to do because it can paralyse you.

We need to remember that verbal abuse is an issue of control; a means of holding power over another person. There are some facts that add some perspective to the abuser's behaviour. Normally in a verbally abusive relationship the abuser denies the abuse all the time. Verbal abuse most often takes place when no one is watching and physical abuse is always preceded by verbal abuse.

You need to remember that if you're under verbal and emotional abuse, make sure that you'll be safe, because physical abuse follows. Normally the verbal abuse becomes more intense over time; it starts to escalate and gets worse. I remember myself, always finding excuses for his behaviour or trying not to make a 'big deal' out of his behaviour and trying to behave normally the next day, but I was getting more hurt through time. I remember how he seemed irritated and angry with me several times a week or sometimes very upset using the silent treatment, so I was being surprised each time. I never knew how my next day with him was going to be, because I never knew which kind of mood he'd be in. Would he be kind the next day? Would he be nice? Would he be angry? Mean? I was always surprised.

When we feel hurt and we try to discuss our feelings, we finish the conversation as if the issue hasn't been fully resolved. We don't feel happy and relieved, nor do we have a feeling that we have solved the problem. I was feeling frequently perplexed and frustrated by his response, because I couldn't get him to understand my intentions and I had a good intention to fix and have solutions for whatever was going on behind his behaviour.

The communication issue in the relationship was the most damaging because I was saying what he thinks I said, and what I heard him say was different.

Sometimes I wondered, what's wrong with me? I shouldn't feel so bad because of his behaviour. But no, he was hurting me! He wasn't sharing his thoughts or plans with me, actually he wasn't much of a planner anyway, always last minute, and so we couldn't plan or dream together, because he usually kept things to himself.

What was going on many times is that it looked like he seemed to take the opposite view of everything that I was talking about or everything that I was mentioning about a friend or a life situation or something about my day as if my views were wrong and his were always right.

I was sometimes wondering if he perceived me as a separate person and I was always afraid to say to him, stop it, or cut it out, or don't talk like that to me. I was always afraid to step up like that. When I was writing letters like that to him or trying to open some lines of communication, because I thought if I'm writing letters, he can read it and think about the information and maybe think about it and maybe come back to me to talk. But what happened is I wasn't able to talk to him and the letters that I was sending to him weren't receiving feedback.

One of the things I learnt from one of my social workers was the feeling of crazy making experience. We need to recognise the crazy making experience, because this is what happens when we get confused and we are still trying to face the reality in front of us, because one thing is certain, once you face reality and you know where you are, it's obvious that you must take action.

The crazy making experience can include feeling lost, not knowing where to turn, or searching, being caught off guard, feeling confused, disorientated or disconnected, feeling off balance, like the earth had been pulled from under our feet all the time.

Usually the abuser will send you a double message, but somehow you'll be fearful of asking for a clarification. If you ask for a clarification, it's probable that he will not answer and walk away and leave you with nothing.

I had suspicions that something was wrong and facing reality drove me to stop denying it and that I must have courage to take action for myself and my daughter. When I say take action, it means being away from each other even if for a while, because the love that I was feeling for him was real and still inside me. Even after everything, I still have this unconditional, universal love that I feel for any person in the world, but more especially for him, because he is the man I decided to marry and live my life and have a family together with, raising our precious daughter. I felt that his behaviour was stopping me from having what I wanted from life. His behaviour was obligating me to take action about something I didn't really want to do.

Verbal abuse is an unprovoked aggression, the abuser is not provoked by anyone, the abuser might consciously or even unconsciously deny what he's doing and when the abuser is not motivated to change, of course the responsibility of recognising verbal abuse rests on the partner.

I remember he was always invalidating my feelings, saying something like, 'You shouldn't feel like that', so I felt my feelings always being ignored. Actually, I wasn't paying much attention to my own feelings. I was so busy paying attention to my daughter's feelings, my daughter's needs and trying to have explanations about his feelings and behaviours that I was forgetting about myself. I knew that if I was trying to share my feelings with him about the aggression or the verbal abuse, I would be absolutely sure that he would invalidate all the things I'm talking about.

When the abuser is exercising power over the abused, he or she wants to show control and dominance. The partner needs to find the light in themselves to recognise and respect their personal power, because their personal power shows up in mutuality and co-creation and coordination. Mutuality is a way of being with another person, which promotes the growth and well being of oneself and the other by means of clear communication and in a particular understanding.

While I was being touched by the reality of my situation I was reading a book by Patricia Evans called *The Verbally Abusive Relationship*. I really recommend this book. Reading that book really opened my eyes, because she explains something that I never knew before and she was talking in one of the chapters about the different realities that the abuser and the partner seemed to believe in. I learnt about the *power over*, those who feel power through dominance and control, which means power over. This means they are living in Reality 1 and those who feel power through mutuality and creativity, that's their personal power, and they are living Reality 2.

It explains that the perpetrator or the abuser is always living in Reality 1 and the partner who is trying to fix the relationship is living in Reality 2. Those two realities cannot meet each other, because they have a totally different perspective about the situation.

When both partners know their personal power and they are complete with themselves, they are mutually supportive and empathetic. Both are living in Reality 2 so they are able to build a very healthy relationship, but of course, we cannot have access to our personal power when we don't know about our feelings, when we don't recognise our feelings. The healthy relationship is based on both partners living in Reality 2, where it's to love oneself and to love the other, to follow ones interests and to encourage the other, to enjoy ones creations and to treasure the others, to value ones self and esteem and the others, to express your enthusiasm into the light of the others and to protect oneself and to comfort the other.

The big difference between a healthy and an abusive relationship is that if the words or the attitude disrespects or devalues the other person, powering over, then that's where they are abusive. In order to validate your feelings, you must have very good self-esteem. You must know your rights, like respect, dignity, appreciation, empathy, kind words, caring, equality, sharing feelings. If your self-esteem is so broken and so small, you'll not be able to recognise your own needs and feelings.

When an abuser or perpetrator is living in his own Reality 1, he probably doesn't know he's living there. He avoids his feelings of powerlessness by controlling and dominating his partner. He's not able to face his feelings, because he's so much in fear of having to deal with his own feelings. Sometimes I was trying to be very warm and open, but he would reject my warmth and openness, because these are the very qualities, which he fears in himself.

These qualities would mean vulnerability and vulnerability is a very scary feeling for an abuser. For those who are reading this book and have never been in an abusive relationship before, you certainly will not understand what it's like.

If you are in an abusive relationship you may have never recognised it and that's happened with many women. They are living in a verbal or emotionally abusive relationship and they think that it's normal, that things will get better, or she'll need to keep quiet and he'll be fine. The partner normally has a good intention, good will and a good heart to try to fix things and will believe anything the abuser will tell her.

Many abusers have been known to say I love you, that, 'No one could love you as much as I do', or 'I just want you to be happy', but that cannot be true. Mutuality and equality is very important for a healthy relationship, but remember, someone who is living in Reality 1 does not have in his world any kind of mutuality or equality, or the skills to provide a healthy relationship. He is likely to blame anyone else for his actions. We will never know what will trigger him and how he will show up: angry or controlling, competitive, jealous, manipulative, explosive or sometimes quiet and withdrawn. These are common signs of verbal abuse.

Normally, they look like very nice guys to our friends and family. Hostility is one of the words that are very connected with the abuse. Lack of intimacy is another thing. What we need to remember is that just because a person doesn't put hands on you, that doesn't' mean they aren't abusive. Abuse is control, blatant disrespect and also hurtful words. Don't settle for emotional abuse thinking it's okay 'just' because it's not physical.

In my case, even living physically separated, I was seeing myself being very loyal behind his back, because my soul was still 'married' so I was being loyal to my heart, my family values, my feelings and my expectations of a family. And I was really hoping that maybe we could, in the future, look back and say, 'Oh, look, we had this experience in the past, but we were both willing to change and were both willing to work hard together in this relationship and we are here, with a healthy relationship today'. That was the illusion I was living before facing the reality. It took me years of observing behaviour and analysing the pattern to really convince me those things was unlikely going to improve. And maybe it was time to bury my heart.

When is the exact moment when we recognise the feeling of trying again or really moving on? When is that moment when you are already so broken inside, that even feeling compassion and sorrow for someone you care so much is not enough to make them realise how much they are destroying themselves, and seriously affecting their significant others' lives?

I knew I have so much love to give, I have light and I am full of life inside my soul. How much more precious time I was going to spend waiting, living and planning life alone with Joahnne while waiting for someone to wake up, stand up, take action, make better decisions, step forward, and walk to the next level of maturity to start to see clearly. That was a thought constantly following me.

We have to get clear in our purpose of life and clear of the junk of our past, influencing our present decisions. When trying to relax, how many voices or people are in there with you? When you want to move forward in your life what scary memories or fears start running in your mind? Well, those negative voices need to be silenced. Clearing out all of those doubts and fears, let the past be the past and bury all those built-in negative feelings that are driving you to make wrong decisions. Make a better choice for the gift that is called 'present'. The future would be different if being wiser in the past. Clearing a white space in our mind to think with the heart will clear the grey clouds and the negative self-talk that is just in our head (not real) or negative emotional memories, so we will see exactly how to act with kindness towards those we love.

We must remember to respect ourselves enough to walk away from anyone that is showing no intention on getting things right or from anything that no longer serve, grow, or make us feel happy. If we aren't being treated with love and respect, we need to check our price tag. Maybe we've marked ourselves down, and that was what I did for a while, being submissive until getting enough. It's us who shows people what our worth is, so better to get off the clearance shelf and put ourselves behind the crystal glass where the valuables are kept.

Avoiding pain will just give you more and bigger pain. We've got to go through the pain to find ourselves behind the broken, to know what makes us tick, to cleanse our heart of memory toxins, to have our soul passions find relief, to get to the stillness, to find out what's real and unreal, and doing it so it will be possible to feel the love flourishing.

That is the blessing that I found behind the reality, when I was touched by reality and facing my fears and really accepting what was going on with me, I knew that it would hurt, but I knew that I will get through and make this with a smile on my face, because I have hope in the future, because I have a faith in myself and I want to provide the best life ever for my daughter as she was always my big why to decide anything. Everything I was doing or not doing was for her best.

We have to remember that our special life is for us and our purpose has nothing to do with the opinions of others. Don't allow others to make you feel small. We come to this world to grow and to explore and to touch the miracles and marvels of life. Our suffering needs to be respected. We can't try to ignore our hurt, because the hurt is real. Instead, we can prove that there is hope through our feeling. Let the hurt soften you instead of hardening you. Let the hurt open doors that wouldn't be open if we weren't living that crisis situation. Let the hurt deliver us love and no hate. Once we understand and accept this, it will obviously be easier to let it go and move on with life.

Chapter 5
Touched by Love

'Between what is said and not meant, and what is meant and not said, most of love is lost.'

– Khalil Gibran

It's not the love that sustains a relationship, but yes it's the way that we relate that sustains the love. I'd like to start this chapter with a passage from the Bible. It says:

> Love is patient, love is kind. It does not envy, it does not boast. It is not proud. It is not rude. It is not self-seeking. It is not easily angered. It keeps no record of wrongs. Love does not delight in evil but rejoices with truth. It always protects, always trusts, always perseveres. Love never fails. But where there are prophecies there will be seeds. Where there are tongues, they will be stilled. Where there is knowledge, it will pass away.
>
> – 1 Corinthians 13:4-8.

I am absolutely sure that the love for my daughter was always my strongest weapon to deal with my hurt feelings and disappointments within my marriage. In order to have her feelings protected, in order to have her happiness protected, I would do anything that was in my power to surround her with the best environment and the best feelings that I could provide.

My love for her compelled me to do what I had to do. My love for my daughter made me stronger in any situation I encountered on my way. For her, I was able to leave if needed and for her I would able to rebuild my relationship with her father and give to him all the love I have for him.

I always believed that the love I have for him inside my core, in my heart, is something that belongs just to him and must be delivered and not kept. Being blocked to deliver such a gift because the other is refusing to receive is frustrating. But through the years what I learnt is that the big love I had inside myself could be transformed into a kind of love that I could use for another purpose, like helping people in need or making me a better person in this world to serve people and to serve my daughter.

It takes courage to be a parent and bravery to love and take care of a child's needs, to be there for them, to care for them, to love them when they push you away. It takes courage to put our own dreams on hold to deal with our own heart and disappointments and just when you think you might be handling the things, you lose your husband. Now you have no choice but to pull it together and care for the most precious, most amazing person you know. Parenting is not for cowards and single parenting is the most courageous actions of love that can exist. It is a daily nonstop giving of your soul.

This book is about my unspoken love and unspoken pain. There is hurt, there is pain. We are all broken hearts at some stage in life. We all have brokenness in this world and we need to pick up our pieces and understand why we have been through such a situation and what we have actually to learn from that. Adults need to cope with disappointment all the time and that's life.

This is all about training; life is a big training room. I believed that when you have an open heart and you're able to receive love, just as open minds are able to receive wisdom and just as open hands are able to receive gifts. The universe will provide love, wisdom, gifts and blessings that we need to turn us into special open souls, to deserve receiving messages of affection and blessings.

I found myself in such a position where I could either let the situation continue destroying the person I knew I was (as I was lost somewhere in the middle of the crisis), or I could step out of the emotional and psychological battle and take action and take back control of my life.

I had been keeping a diary for some time, and this really saved my life in so many ways, because it was the thing that helped me to see the repetitive destructive patterns. I cannot emphasise enough the value of keeping a diary, because in the end it helped me to prove to myself that this wasn't my fault, as he wanted me to believe it. At that moment when I came to my senses, and could finally face the reality of the situation I could only then take action. By that time I was very well advised about the fact that the consequence of not taking action would highly affect the emotional development of our daughter. How I could continue to be the dedicated loving mother I was while living under this distress, unpredictability, rejection and fear? My daughter's future wellbeing was more important than keeping my marriage. How could I be helpful to people in need or how could I be a happy woman when my energy levels were so low because they were already used up? Allowing people to destroy our soul has nothing to do with being a good and loyal wife or even a good person.

There are limits and I took a long time to learn to put into practise some boundaries. I took a bit of time to understand that I would best help my daughter and myself from a position of strength than from a position of weakness. For years I was trying to save everyone in my family, but the reality was that it wasn't possible, some people are going to destroy themselves, no matter how much we give them time or opportunity and they cannot even see it. Some people have their lives, full of chaos, anxiety and dysfunction and if we allow it, they will consciously or unconsciously bring the pain to your life, making your life miserable. There are others who do not destroy themselves or just think they're not destroying themselves but instead survive through destruction of others. These are the users.

The deep motherly love is the automatic instinctive sense of protecting our children from harm. My turning point, being touched by the love for my daughter, was when I realised that we had a right to be loved and safe.

If we can rescue our children from experiencing an abusive environment or watching their mother treated unfairly, they will not have to spend a lifetime searching and trying to recover, or repair once they are adults, and will not be emotionally broken from all the painful things they would go through, if staying. On top of that, they will feel great about themselves and consequently be able to offer other people around them a healthy and enjoyable relationship.

The international bestselling book by Erich Fromm, *The Art of Loving* says, 'Love is an activity not a passive effect. It is a standing in and not a falling for. Love is inherently bound with responsibility, respect, appreciation, giving and sharing. Love is an art, meaning one improves through concentration, practise and in understanding your own strengths and weaknesses.' Love impacts our interactions with both our friends and strangers, as well as influencing our decisions about what we share, do and say. It affects our perspectives to new information and tolerance for difference. Wayne Dyer used to say that, 'If you have anything in your heart, that's anything other than love, you've got to get it out'.

Part of respecting and appreciating everything from people and nature is opening yourself to giving it your full attention. I find it useful to minimise my conscious thoughts and allow myself to fully submerge in the moment. This helps me then to answer as an honest human being. The truth is ironically that many try to deny their love, to deny their connection to the world around them and their shared responsibility for the future. Love is not a form of ownership or possessiveness; it is on the contrary a fostering of growth.

Love is one of the ultimate joys of life. One of the deepest and most fulfilling connections to the world. Understanding your emotions or loving does definitely not have to be an irrational act.

If I could give my daughter three things, it would be the confidence to always know her self-worth, the strength to chase her dreams and the ability to know how truly deeply loved she is.

Real love is about opening your heart to the unlovable things or the unlovable person. Real gratitude is giving thanks when things are not good. Real generosity is sharing when you have very little and real courage makes the impossible possible with real faith.

Parenting is the hardest job you will ever have. It's a lifelong, 24/7 vocation where you are constantly on call in crisis mode and required to make executive decisions. From appropriate snack choices to learning manners, on the spot without an instruction manual, all the while battling waves of fear, doubt and regret.

Who could blame you for feeling like you may literally lose your mind for the slightest reason? Love is about kindness, by being beautiful and kind, you're doing your part to create a more beautiful world. When you are kind to people, you become a force for good and you're teaching everyone to do the same, because they are watching you. Be a role model to your child. Being a role model to your child means that you are acting the way that you'd like her to learn. People know love when they feel it. Your heart speaks to their heart. People don't care what you say, only how you make them feel. Try to create pleasure in every connection you have in your life.

Your life will change forever if you decide to be kind to the world, because what's going to happen is that the world will be kind back to you and if not, it's not your fault.

You can touch many hearts with your kindness and your smile and when people are touched by your heart and love, they feel great and they believe in themselves and they'll be forever grateful for you if you make them feel nice and feel great.

All of us here in this world are created for feeling and thinking. We must devote our lives not only to material things, but also to kindness and helping each other. There is no greater intelligence than kindness and empathy. Kindness is the supreme intelligence.

It's wise to teach our children how to empower themselves in the seven areas of life. Not just that, but for us in order to grow too. Here are the seven areas:

1. Mentally: Look after your mind.

2. Physically: Looking after your body.

3. Socially: Looking after your relationships.

4. Financially: Looking after your money and your needs.

5. Vocationally: Looking after your career and your purpose. What are you going to share with this world? How can you help this world to be better?

6. Family: Looking after your closest people. Love them, because they are in your family, not as an accident. We are families, because there is a purpose behind that. Even if you cannot see the purpose that doesn't mean it's not there. Be responsible with your family members. When I say family members it means people from blood or from heart, because sometimes we have family members on a spiritual level. Don't make your family suffer because of your ego. A man needs to step up as a husband, a father, a partner and provider and as a leader of a family based on love and intimacy. Provider of security, making sure his family is safe emotionally and financially. A partner is someone who takes part in an undertaking with another, with all the responsibility, which a relationship requires.

7. Spiritually: Your spiritual development is one of the most important investments you can give to yourself. It's why you are here. We are a soul with this body, we are not just a body with a soul.

I called this book, *Touched by Love*, because I really had the hope and the wish to share with the world how much I was touched by the love of the community, by the love of people, by the love of God and by the love of my daughter and myself and the love of the world. I was touched by love all the way through my crisis situation. It is not about writing a book, but the person I become in the process afterwards, liberating suppressed truths and healing them, through owning my story and as a consequence be able to serve people.

Even in the middle of chaos, I was thrilled on receiving blessings all the time, even while living in a women's refuge, twice, with my daughter while we were temporarily homeless, I was happy for the blessing to be there.

When you have such love inside your mind and your heart, you start to attract love from other people too. The world starts to move around, to get your things done, and get your needs met. I remember having friends come over to give me stuff for the kitchen and the rooms, I remember a friend of mine giving me a new bed for my daughter and I was able to rebuild a full house with everything we needed. I was feeling that feeling of abandonment from him, but I was filled with love that I was receiving from the world.

And I always felt so blessed that I wasn't in a worse situation, because when I was living in a woman's refuge in Lane Cove, I saw many women suffering in situations that I couldn't even believe could exist in the world. My story was pretty sad and traumatic, but while I was listening to those women living with me, it would really break my heart every day. This is why it was important to tell my story to help people overcome domestic violence.

One of the books I really loved to read was about the Five Love Languages. The five love languages explain the languages of words of affirmation, quality time, receiving gifts, acts of service and physical touch. Each person in this world relates to more with one or another of the five love languages. When I relate to other people I express my love for them through these love languages. This is what makes me unique and special to them.

I express how I love people through words, kind words, thoughtful words, encouraging and gentle words, words that lift up and make people feel like they are the most important person in the world. I also express how I love people through acts of service. I am involved in many committees and volunteer work, I am always trying to be available to help out my friends, at the school, or in the community, and I even host a small Brazilian spiritualist group here on the Central Coast. In relationships I need physical touch. My daughter and I are always hugging each other to affirm our love, affection and sense of connection and in a relationship physical touch is so important to affirm my commitment to my partner.

In my marriage I was not receiving any affirmation of love for me. I needed this so much and my spiritual tank was completely empty. In a relationship you are supposed to feel loved, honoured, cherished and special. Because I was living with a narcissist I was not able to communicate my deep need for love, in the way that I could understand it. It takes two people to equally contribute to a united loving and peaceful family life. If one partner cannot do this, or is unwilling to try to understand how to do this, then the relationship cannot thrive. In my situation, not only was I not receiving any affirmation of love, I experienced verbal and emotional abuse, a lack of support and withdrawal in the form of extended periods of silence that could last for weeks.

He didn't know how much I needed him. I wasn't able to show him or he wasn't able to realise how much I needed him, supporting me, beside me, holding my hand, affirming his love and showing that I was still his special one. I wanted him to know how much I needed him to be the stronger one, the emotional leader of our relationship; so that I could be weak sometimes because I knew he would take over to take care about us. He wasn't able to show me that. All of this meant that I was feeling obligated to leave, obligated to walk away from something that I always wanted to give to my daughter, what I didn't have as a child with my own parents. A united family with my husband my marriage and my daughter meant everything to me. But in the end because of the situation I felt like had no choice.

'Love one another deeply, from the heart.'

– 1 Peter 1:22

Chapter 6

Touched by Decision

'Decisions are the hardest moves to make when it is a choice between what you want and what is right. Once you make a decision, the universe conspires to make it happen.'

– Rhonda Byrne

Should I stay or should I leave? Try harder or give up? It is the biggest question for a woman in an unhealthy relationship. It was the decision that was challenging me daily after becoming aware and facing the hard reality with honesty. For those who do choose to leave an unhealthy relationship, they really enable themselves to have that power of choice and they take that leap with no fear and allow themselves that freedom that we should all have in our lives.

When you make a decision to leave because you realise that it's the right thing to do, you must ensure the safety of yourself, and your children. Remember that you are being the role model for them, they are watching you, and learning what and how you accept to be treated or not accept to be treated and how you behave so they build a belief system that will be intrinsic on their own subconscious for the future of their own relationships. Educating your children as an example will determine that they will not become an abusive partner in the future or experience the abuse themselves. Ultimately, the biggest goal of making a decision is for them to have a better life, feel safe, happy and fulfilled and to have an amazing journey to increase self-worth. That way, you attract positive things in life.

Remember that domestic violence is not a form of men losing control; it is an attempt at *gaining* control. Most acts of abuse are premeditated, occurring behind closed doors. It may seem as though the abuser is losing control because of his angry behaviour. To that end, most abusers are good manipulators. They know how to convince others and their victims that they are not at fault for their actions. The physical and mental abuse often escalates the longer a person stays in an unhealthy relationship and ultimately the children of those women being abused end up being abusers themselves, or the worst case scenario is that they attract the partner that abuses them.

Most abusive relationships go through cycles – from tension building to an active battering incident, leading to the honeymoon or "remorseful" stage. This pattern, called the "Cycle of Violence", came from the women's movement in the 1970s. The idea has changed over the years because many women found that their relationships did not go through all or each of these phases. For some people there is no "honeymoon" phase. Others do not see the tension building. Women's rights activists today have changed the model, renaming it the "Campaign of Violence." The new name suggests that the violence is ongoing and multi-faceted, taking on a variety of forms.

Realising those trials and tribulations in the inventory of our lives, we are going to make mistakes, but we trust our life to God, the foundation of strength and guidance, to guide us to the bright side of decisions.

Have a close look at your life and work out whether you will stay or go. After all, some relationships are salvageable and that is something that only you can decide based on your partners behaviour and genuine effort instead of your hopes and your love.

There are many reasons why women stay in an abusive relationship with partners who hurt them, but some of common reasons may be:

1. Lack of social support or feeling isolated.

2. Limited financial resources as financial control is the biggest weapon of the partner.

3. Limited work experience.

4. Child custody and support may also be a big factor as she fears for the safety of the children.

5. Fear of being alone, homeless, unable to provide for their children.

6. The pressure of family or community plus the feeling of shame.

7. Believing that they are "causing" the abuse (crazy making factor), believe it or not they will often find themselves walking on eggshells and trying desperately to avoid behaviours they believe will cause the abuse.

8. Sometimes the relationship may seem healthy on many occasions.

9. They may be afraid of provoking additional violence as revenge from the partner, especially when that would affect their children.

10. Distrust of police and authorities.

11. Believing abuse is normal.

12. Cultural or religious reasons.

13. Language barrier.

14. Disability.

When you realise you're in crisis, you'd like to know what's going on. As soon as you are aware of what's going on, you need to face the reality. After facing reality you can assess the situations of love and non-love inside the reality you are living. Next step, you must make a decision for your future. Marriage, separation and divorce are considered to affect you in the same way as grief cycles for the death of a loved one, but that pain doesn't stop you from feeling worthy of achieving a better quality life. Experiencing separation and/or divorce is related to the death of people's dreams, death of commitment, the end of what they had been planning happily for their children. On many occasions, self-esteem and confidence will drop and the need to recreate yourself again will arise instantly.

In particular, when the marriage breakdown happens due to a traumatic unhealthy situation as we are exploring here, the frustration and resentment will increase considerably, on top of the circumstances to be faced, as well as the feelings of being treated unfairly. One of the hardest decisions you'll ever face in life is choosing whether to walk away or try harder, and how to understand that trying harder will only push you further down from where you already are.

I was sadly watching my husband hopelessly confused, with his mind full of darkness and totally closed, with his heart hardened toward me and with no sense of shame, acting thoughtlessly and walking far from the gift God kindly gave to him, being powerless, tricked by evil influence. A man who loves his wife will be showing love toward himself and will receive the respect from his wife. That wasn't happening at all.

Leaving home

Big courage is required to leave your 'comfort zone' that wasn't actually comfortable anymore, leaving your belongings behind with a baby in your arms and without any money, going to a place that is foreign. But when that day arrived, I was going to feel safer in any place, with any people than spending one more day at home. I just remember sleeping on the floor of my daughter's room (the sacred space for us) the night before and praying in tears, 'God please get me out of here.' That was how scared I was about the last events. I was so frightened (for me and for Joahnne) and so broken and exhausted that I would accept to go anywhere as far away possible from what I was experiencing. Be careful what you ask! It may happen! The next morning I was out of my home.

I didn't know what to expect next, but I was filled with assurance that I was making the best decision available because if I didn't, I would be allowing my soul to die inside my own home and exposing our daughter to that unsafe and unpredictable environment. How to be your best as a person and as a mother, when you are living under such a destructive and toxic environment? I wouldn't allow my daughter to stay one more minute around that unhealthy situation where she was seeing her mother stressed, living in a protective and survival mode all the time, and yet trying to play, sing and dance with her every single day.

By that night before, I was filled with more than enough evidence and reasons to feel strong to make changes and start to use my legal rights without feeling guilt, to protect me and remove our daughter from the unsustainable situation. The last three months I was writing in my diary the list of countless evidence of Domestic Violence, because I needed to really believe to take action without feeling that I would be 'unfair' to 'him'. The emotional evidences I was already experiencing for two years I've already described. The financial control was getting extremely ridiculous with numerous consequences, not just for me but for our daughter too. He was refusing to buy baby wipes and I was begging to buy nappies. One day I took a photo from the fridge, because it was empty. My emails were being tracked. The physical abuse did happen with pushing, hurting my foot, getting my neck against the wall. And during the last months the verbal abuse was very low with name calling such as nail-head, ignorant, pig, liar pig, stupid, and worst later saying to my parents that I was a prostitute, calling my family 'gang' and other black mail.

Just days before I left, my father received a weird email with FYI copy to me saying that I was being 'returned' (as a damaged product, yeah?) and that I would soon return to Brazil and he was going to stay in Australia with Joahnne as I wasn't going to be able to receive my Australian residence if separating. Little did he know that later, while living in the refuge, I was the one signing a document to dismiss his charges at court, saving him from having his residence application denied.

When men are so angry and blind, out of self-control, they can't really see the ridiculous and low attitude. They may really believe they are right and the victim. They also don't care or aren't able to put themselves in their child's feelings to think a moment about how he might be hurting his own child, if hurting the mother. It doesn't matter. Their ego is so big that the only thing that they can see in front of their eyes is the urgency to win a battle created by them in their mind. It will not matter who they are hurting. The focus is how to destroy the partner that petulantly decided to step up against his 'rules'. Using children to reach or to hurt the spouse are unfortunately very common from the abusers.

The circumstance on the next early morning was just the catalyst for the change to take place. We had a fight, and for the first time instead of being quiet, afraid or passive, I reacted and faced him. On that morning, his sarcasm and irony seemed dangerous to me. He left home calling me a pig while walking downstairs. I called the domestic violence police to report the physical incident in the morning and they arrived soon. All the facts were taken. One of my friends came to rescue Joahnne for me and take her to childcare while I was coping with the situation. Joahnne got distressed and left crying but I knew she was going to be in the caring hands with one of my best friends and have a great day at childcare while I was going to have a long, exhausting day grabbing my things to leave.

The policeman that arrived to rescue me called the station and they said that surprisingly he was at the police station trying to write a report against me for the fight that we had had that morning. They had one event number before, so Dee Why Police charged him straight away and took him to Manly for a full day while giving me time to move out. I had friends coming over with a little truck to move out some belongings, Joahnne's belongings, and kitchen appliances that I could sell and have some money to be able to provide for Joahnne in the first days.

Later he funnily wrote I did steal from him. That afternoon the police officer called me to ask if I was already in a safe place and if I had already picked up Joahnne from childcare, so they could release him. They informed me that the police officer had charged him, and put an interim Apprehended Domestic Violence Order in place. An Apprehended Domestic Violence Order, which is made to protect victims of domestic violence from harm. It means that for the time of the Order the perpetrator is not allowed to harm the victim, and if this does occur, it is a criminal offence. In order to support victims of domestic violence, Women's Domestic Violence Court Advocacy Services are funded to assist women in Apprehended Domestic

Violence Order (ADVO) matters; so the perpetrator wouldn't approach the victim for determined time decided by court. Joahnne's name was also written in the document.

I had two nights at my girlfriend's home in Dee Why, hiding and scared. She had been supporting me emotionally for many months. On Monday morning, with my car totally full, I drove Joahnne and I to our next adventure, moving to the women's refuge in Lane Cove. We lived in the women's refuge for three months and then my amazing social caseworker secured for me a very good two-room unit under government housing.

Joahnne and I were being carefully protected from the one who supposed to be protecting and nurturing us. I was slowly taking challenge by challenge and rebuilding our life with a new house, filled with love, filled with compassion and harmony, and filled with support from people I never knew existed before. I had earth angels called friends and strangers, taking action and campaigning to support our basic needs. I was so blessed, humble and grateful to deserve such a blessing from the universe.

What is it like to live in the women refuge?

It is a safe place where everything is taken care of for you, from immigration law to lawyers, kid's services, art therapy, counselling, emotional support, court matters, financial matters and much more. I was very lucky to be allocated to Lane Cove. Just two days later I had to drive to Manly to meet him in court for the case to be heard. It was a difficult moment where I had opposite feelings of fear of him and deep compassion with a deep desire to help him in that difficult moment. I was very vulnerable, confused feeling love/compassion and so much fear for the one who was giving me such a hard time in life. The court decided for the Apprehended Domestic Violence Order again and I drove back to the Refuge in Lane Cove.

No matter how I was feeling or what was happening around me, I was inspiring people around me, being always positive, supporting the mothers living in the refuge with kindness, because I was always being grateful and feeling so blessed. I really believe that my deep faith always saved me when I most needed it, because it did! You can have a go to practice your faith in many different ways, but serving people is the most rewarding one, as it is the main message from Jesus. I call my faith God, but you can call it the Higher Power, Universe, Buddha, inner light, or whatever you like; the name is not the most important thing, the important thing is that you must humbly believe there's a higher power coordinating and managing the universe and those energies of life will bring what is supposed to be in your life.

I had a childhood memory of being separated from my mother due to the problems my parents experienced. So, I was going to make sure Joahnne wasn't going to experience this trauma, as I was almost 100% of her care since she was born and symbol of safety and love. When I received threats about separating Joahnne from me, I committed myself that no matter what, I was going to make sure she will be protected from this risk, and avoid her to be used to target me. And each time they will meet, it would be a positive experience, avoiding messing with her mind. I was fighting to make sure that whenever they saw each other again it was with love, peace and a positive experience for my daughter.

Deep in my heart I know how much he loves her and I never meant to get her away from him, but protect her from the toxic emotional state he was living in at that time. For a while, after I left, his choices weren't positive and healthy, so what I had to do was to make sure he had time off to cool down and put himself together first to be in a better mindset and then be able to give to her the best he could. So the Apprehended Domestic Violence Order worked very well to achieve that timeframe. I knew in my heart he was hurting as well, but at the point my main job now was to take care of just Joahnne and myself, I couldn't be responsible for his feelings, I had enough on my plate.

I had another turbulent 24h of big stress when my social caseworker had to relocate us to another women's refuge because he knew where we were. That was hard! I had to leave from where we were settled and safe, with all our belongings, to a strange place and I didn't have a good feeling about it. When I arrived, I hated the place and decided that I was not going to stay there. After serving dinner to Joahnne, I realised I left my mobile charger in Lane Cove and called to pick it up next morning. As I told myself that I wasn't going to spend one more hour at that place with my daughter, I did something crazy. Before dawn, I packed my car again and we left, leaving the room key under the door, and drove more than an hour back to Lane Cove praying that my friend living there would open the door for me, and let me stay until the managers arrived. She did, my room code wasn't changed yet and I could spend the rest of the night back in Lane Cove. That was totally against the rules and I believe that that never happened before. The next day I was begging the manager and my wonderful social worker to let me stay there, assuring them that he wasn't going to look for us there even if knowing where we were, that was due to a mistake made by another organisation. Blessed I was again, as they decided to let me stay and continue to be cared for by my super professional and wise social caseworker. Melanie was one of the angels in my life and I am forever grateful for her service and friendship.

While living in the women's refuge, I had the opportunity to get to know amazing women from different cultures also experiencing their own crisis situations. Some of them with heartbreaking stories that easily made me feel sorry for the world we live in. Strong women defending their honour and the safety of their children from the ones who are supposed to be protecting them. I knew inside my soul that I was living a special opportunity of growth and from here I wouldn't be silent anymore. My initial desire of writing a book arose from that. Despite the emotional breakdown I was having and all the problems I was being forced to solve, Joahnne and I had a very special time living there, feeling happy, free, protected, nurtured and cared for.

The Brighter Future was one of the organisations that made the big difference in providing the best social environment for Joahnne. They paid her childcare so I could continue driving to Dee Why to keep working as a waitress at the RSL. They were paying for nappies, clothes and extras for her.

I was surviving with help from Salvation Army, St Vincent de Paul Society and Brighter Future. I sold a lot of the stuff I could get from my home and that helped.

At that time I wasn't an Australian resident as I left before our family application was approved, so I didn't have the right to receive the government pension but Melanie applied for a special benefit pension, and from May I was approved to receive about AUD$600 fortnightly.

Later she applied for Child Support (CSA) for Joahnne to receive her rights as his daughter, which was calculated at AUD$90 per week. It was something to make him responsible for. Joahnne was great, always having a good time, as I was making sure to transform everything into a fun and positive experience, making sure to be there for her 100%. She loved to live in the women's refuge with others children, she was having fun. Joahnne didn't have a strong emotional bond with him, due to the way we were living, therefore that helped a lot at this time.

If you are considering leaving a domestic violence situation, here are some questions you can consider in your head: Have you had enough yet? What's your happiness worth to you? What's your kids' happiness and safety worth? Are you ready to go off the sentiments you feel, the anger, the resentment, the disappointment you feel? How about low self-esteem and low libido? Do you want your mojo back? Moving forward can take time and for some people. Getting confidence back for yourself will require consistent work. Believe you are loveable, worthy, beautiful and smart, this will help to block anyone from destroying your self-esteem and you will feel empowered and able to dream again.

At some point, in the middle of your pain, you will need to make a decision for yourself, for your kids, for your marriage, for your situation. If the abusive partner is not able to take responsibility, you must take responsibility for you and your kids. Take the power of responsibility in your hands and make decisions of what's going to be better for your future, instead of stagnating in a situation that's not going anywhere. Sometimes we separate because of the kids, to give them a better love environment that isn't possible with mum and dad together.

Here are the five benefits that I discovered when making my decision.

1. Freedom.

2. Choice and self-empowering.

3. Safety for self and children.

4. Role model.

5. Fulfilment and own worth.

Do you know that there are statistics showing that on average, a woman will leave an abusive relationship **seven times** before she leaves for good? That is how serious the cycle of abuse is and how tricky the emotional situation evolved between the partner and the abuser is. This means that a woman's heart believes again and again until the bucket of hope is completely empty or until she exposes herself and the kids to so much pain that the amount of pain will finally make her realise that she is the one who needs to change her mindset and move on. After I left, while living in the women's refuge with Joahnne, this particular statistic shocked me deeply and I remember saying to myself that I wouldn't allow myself to be part of those same statistics. In Australia around one in four women have experienced severe physical violence by an intimate partner, and of the total domestic violence homicides worldwide, about seventy five per cent of the victims were killed as they attempted to leave the relationship. Still yet other research shows that seventy three per cent of male abusers were also abused as children.

To be able to give up on someone we love so much, requires strength and hope. No one wants to give up on a relationship that we dreamed for and no one wants to give up on someone that we believed we loved so much. Sometimes we are forced to make hard decisions, by suffering.

For me I felt like I was being forced to leave someone I have so much love, affection and compassion, and stop believing that I could, just with my strength, heal the relationship and be able to keep my family together. It's easy to judge and say, *never give up*, once you have been there. Eventually you begin to realise that life is too short and your powers to teach, heal and influence are limited. You can teach influence and heal yourself, but you can't control other people and they have their own choices and under their choices, they will live the consequence of that.

It's hard to accept that the pain and dysfunction requires more than I have to give. I can't hand my whole life and soul over to someone who doesn't even care about their own. How can you help someone who's living in self-destruction for so long? Sometimes the only option is to let it go. Some of the people we love the most are going to destroy themselves and there is nothing we can do about it. Some people are inclined to have attraction and their inevitable undoing is heartbreaking to watch and some things you will never understand and that's because we live in different realities.

As much as we love someone, we can't make their decisions or live their lives for them. They must make the hard decisions all on their own. In many cases, the disaster is already in play. It's the emotion because of the past actions and the consequences are coming and there's nothing we can do about it. It hurts to watch. It's awful. Letting go is an excruciating heartbreak, mourning the death of what once was.

When we do let someone go and perhaps we still feel some kind of guilt because of it, it's time to wake up and let you be touched by your decision with confidence and see the blessing of forgiving yourself and beginning to heal from inside.

It doesn't matter if you are letting go for the sake of you or for the sake of someone (like your children), this will be your confirmation. What you need to remember is that no matter how badly someone treats you, never stoop down to their level. Remain calm, stay strong and walk away if you need to, even if it's for a short period to balance yourself. Even when people are clearly toxic and abusive, people will agree on cutting them off and getting out of their lives. You don't need a reason to move someone out of your life. A person doesn't need to be toxic for you to get rid of them. You can get rid of any person for any reason; it doesn't matter if they are a saint. If you don't like their vibe or you are uncomfortable or you're feeling that they're out of sync with your life path, you have the right to let them go.

Being a gatekeeper in your own life is crucial. Who you align yourself with is always the paramount consideration of your life. Learning to move people out of the rings of your constant cycles quickly and neatly is a vital skill. Protect your energy and preserve the nucleus of your inner cycle for those who you share or have a destiny with. There is hardly anything more limiting or empowering than whom you allow to stay in your life. Get over the guilt or be a slave to guilt, it's your choice.

I remember I was saying to myself many years ago, never again, never again will I find myself in this situation or beat myself up because of my past mistakes. Never again will I give up on my dream because of what someone else has said or because I've been rejected or experienced failure or a setback. Never again will I not give my all or go all out or represent myself as a powerless, weak, victim because of some tragedy that I've experienced. Never again will I go back to a life, a lie, a relationship or a situation that doesn't represent the best in me. I am better than this, bigger than this, stronger than this.

It is important to remind ourselves that we shouldn't let one temporary situation be the cause of making a permanent decision about new possibilities for the future. We can dare to be great despite how we feel at the moment. One very important step in the process of making decisions for our kids and our life is to face all the fears and the hidden denials. If we keep hiding from reality in the process of being touched by decision, we will be not able to progress and grow. The bible says that you can't heal a wound by saying it's not there. If we do not face our denials, what can happen? Facing our emotions and understanding our feelings is the key of freedom.

Anxiety is another sign of denial. Anxiety causes us to waste precious energy running from our past and worrying about and dreading the future. If you don't stop denials, you will negate growth. We cannot grow and recover until we are ready to step out of our denial into the truth.

That was happening in my relationship. We kept denying our situation and pretending that it wasn't happening. By doing that you will isolate yourself from the higher power, the power of the universe, your spirit of connection and from God. One of the most important things that happens if you keep denying your situation is that you will be alienated from your relationships. The false belief that denial will protect you from your pain is false! In reality, denial will allow the pain to fester and grow and turn shame into guilt. Stepping out of denial and stepping into your higher power, unconditional love and grace will lead you to your better future, for sure.

As soon as you decide about what you're going to do in the next step, if you decide to leave, even for a temporary period to get things sorted and maybe fixed, you need to remember to have a plan. Plan to live safely and get help. I left my relationship twice; the first was a very traumatic running away and the second time was a very calm and assertive decision. To rebuild myself, I decided to invest in personal and spiritual development, exposing me to the work of healing through social work and therapy, picking up my emotional pieces and brokenness and getting my feelings together again on track, trying to understand myself better and also to get to know myself better. I was feeling confused, I didn't know who I was anymore for some time.

Of course while I was questioning myself about my future decisions, many doubts was popping up like:

1. What if he doesn't want to get help? In this case the relationship is unlikely to change and the problems will escalate.

2. What if his threats and hitting is keeping me scared? Look for a specialised support. It's free and you can get lots of information about that.

3. What if I make the wrong decision? There is no wrong or right decision. Follow your instinct, your heart and your gut. Where do you want to be? What is the best for your children and yourself? Remember to think about what you don't want in your life. That will help you know what you want and what you need.

I was asking myself:

- What is motivating the need for my decision?
- What would happen if I don't take any decision?
- Who and how will my decision impact?
- What supporting information do I have to validate the inclinations driving my decisions?
- Here I want to talk about a few options, because some people will choose to stay for a little more and reach for help. Just remember that very often, the abuser will say that there is nothing wrong with them and they tell you to get help just for you, as their reaction is to always blame you for his behaviour. Please do not believe it, in any healthy relationship, both partners must be willing to reach and solve their problems with maturity and proactive actions to protect their families and their love, if it is genuine. Finally, the ones who will choose to take action and leave will do that after realising that the situation is definitely not salvageable.

I remember one thing that I learnt: what kills you is not the bite of the snake as nobody ever died from a snakebite. It's just a bite, right? We can be bitten many times if we are in the jungle. What kills you is not the bite, it's the venom. The poison that stays with you and circulates within you long after the bite and the poison will kill you unless you find a way to release it, so release the damage on your life. Figure out how to turn it into a lesson for your situation. Transform what was toxic into medicine and in this way you'll be turning the decision of the moment that looks like a crisis to you, into a moment of blessing and majesty in your life. Believe that there is magic around you and magic, which transforms life, connects dots, moves mountains and forecasts events that shock us.

Your imagination is a powerful place, so be careful where you point your imagination, because it can also stop you in your tracks, bring fear, get you lost, and break you down. Transform your imagination into thoughts of blessing that will drive you to the right path.

One of the important things you should consider is: what would happen to your children if you don't leave the abusive relationship and keep living with the perpetrator, hoping everyday that things will be better and he will start to communicate and be loving? Actually my decision was more based on the good will and the love that I have for my daughter and how much I didn't want her to be around that unhealthy environment. How much I wanted to be the best role model ever for her, which I wasn't able to be because of my emotional breakdown.

What happens with babies and toddlers? What happens with children 4-12 years old and what happens with young people?

Babies and toddlers are deeply affected by what is happening in a domestic violence situation even if they are in the womb, and the effects can be permanent where they are unable to feel accepted, loved and valued their whole lives. A reliable and positive relationship is vital to help children manage the stress and trauma in their lives. Joahnne was two years old when I left our environment for the first time and I was lucky enough to protect her from any harm that could happen. I was always helping her, supporting her in any of her needs and luckily we were in such a bonded relationship, as I was always her primary carer.

It didn't matter how I was feeling, I was always ready for her. Always ready to support her and give to her all the happiness, all the good and bright that was around our life. Each negative point arising, I turned it into a positive one. It is like playing a happy game, where you choose your experience of a situation. If your toddlers are having eating problems, nightmares, aggression, withdrawal, headaches or greater irritability, please look for a professional therapist for this child. And help them to find a way to deal with their emotions.

Children from 4-12 years old, preschool and primary aged children are affected as they are developing their emotional selves. They can have issues managing emotions, and display impulsive behaviours in interactivity and aggression, not appreciating others' feelings and learning difficulties. For children in this age range parents are very important role models. If you don't leave the situation, you are making your children unsafe and believing that aggression and force is the best way to get what they want and feeling frightened and getting abused is a normal part of a relationship.

Adolescence is the launching pad for establishing their adult identity whilst they are facing important issues such as sexuality, responsibility and independence. This is a critical time as living with an abusive parent will severely interfere with this important life process, and make it difficult for them to establish healthy relationships of their own.

I know that women would say they stay in the unhealthy relationship 'because of the children'. But in reality you must consider that perhaps you must leave the unhealthy relationship 'because of the children' so you will be able to give them a healthy loving environment, being a role model of safe and loving parenting and giving them opportunity to form healthy relationship of their own.

There are some indicators that you may notice and if you do, look for professional help to support your children's needs. This should not be regarded as conclusive indicators, nor should they be ignored.

1. Tiredness: sometimes children are kept awake by the situation at home; they are likely to have disturbed nights, anticipation of the fight or directly because of it.

2. Sleep problems: there can be sleeping disorders such as bedwetting or frightening nightmares.

3. Timidity: children living with abusive environments may be fearful and timid because they live in fear. They may cower in threatening or menacing situations, or physically freeze in situations where they may not trust easily.

4. Aggression: children who live with violence often learn to be aggressive and copy violent behaviour observed at home. Behaviour can be quite extreme, like pushing furniture over or throwing toys.

5. Withdrawal: children who live with abusive environments sometimes withdraw and avoid eye contact and avoid communication of any kind. They may take extra time to settle to a new routine or become used to new stuff, particularly if they have had to flee from a violent home, leaving precious things behind.

6. Lack of trust: it may have been impossible for them to build a sense of trust in the home environment and as a result they may be tentative and suspicious in the new environment. Withdrawal can result in poor social relations; poor physical and mental competence and conclusions about learning difficulties can be wrongly reached.

7. Eating behaviours: children living under abusive relationships may either lose their appetite or eat excessively; they may grab food, steal or even hide food.

8. Health: some indicators can be related to living in an abusive relationship. This includes stomach-aches, headaches, asthma, skin disorders and disorders like stuttering, wetting or soiling things.

As you've been reading this chapter there may still be doubts that can pop up in your mind that I have not addressed yet, but the most common three things I get asked is, what if I'm way too scared to leave, because there's a lot of threats, even on my life? Or what if my partner doesn't want to get help, even if I want to give him a second chance? Then, what if I actually make the wrong decision?

Let's look at those in a little bit of depth.

If you're too scared due to threats, what I would say is to start educating yourself. Start looking for support in your community and look for that support privately. Get as much information as you possibly can to help you understand stuff, because fear is about the unknown, not so much about what is going on around you.

Secondly, if your partner doesn't want to get help, it's time to actually realise that the relationship is unlikely to change and the behaviour is most likely going to escalate. That is what was happening to me. Even when you decide to get help, you should always be cautious that things might go back to the old way, but to give the person a good chance to show that they want to change.

Last of all, about making decisions, in life there really are no right or wrong decisions and we always make the perfect decisions for where we are. I would say, just listen to your heart, follow your gut and do what you want to do according to where you want to get to in your life. What is your purpose? What is best for you and your children?

And don't worry if sometimes your heart needs more time to accept what your mind already knows. But remember the 3 C's of life: Choice, Chances and Changes. You must make a choice to take a chance or your life will never change.

Next chapter we're going to talk about community and I will tell you how I was touched by the love of the community and the connections and network I built through the crisis situation. How the community and services helped me to understand my situation and help my decisions building a safe plan to be able to have my decision made and making me believe that I was going to be okay.

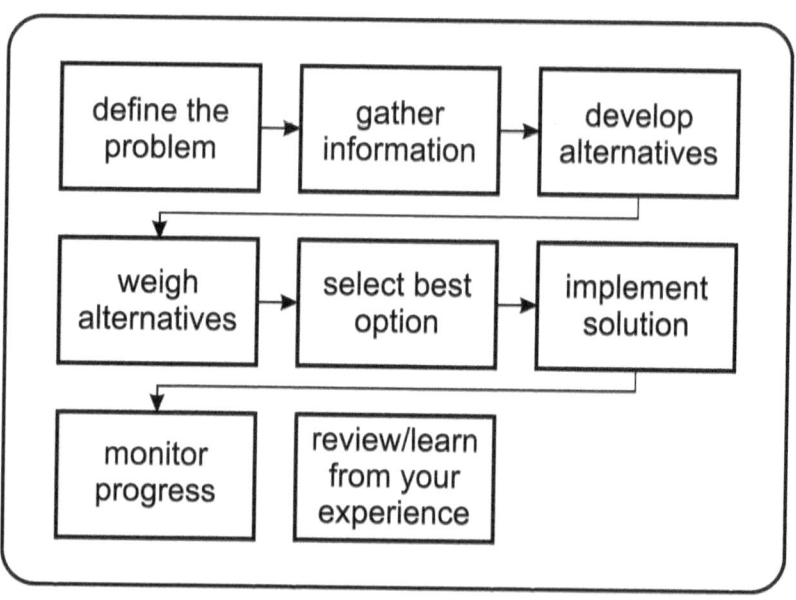

Chapter 7
Touched by Community

'You won't understand the incredible power of community until you're a part of one.'

– Luciane Sperling

The doers, the believers and thinkers, but most of all, surround yourself with those who see greatness within you, even when you don't see it yourself. In this chapter I would like to share how the power of community touched me through my journey.

I wouldn't have achieved all the goals and all the basic needs I was covering if it wasn't for people in the community and organisations. I love Australia. People whom I never knew and who were ready to give me a hand to rebuild my life. When you find yourself feeling alone and abandoned by your partner, working so hard to provide for your lovely children, sometimes you can feel scared about the future, even if the future may be the next minute or years to come.

Remember, you are not alone, ever. As Pope Francisco said, 'There is no such thing as single mothers, because being a mother is not a relationship status'. Being a mother is a love giving, blessed status, but when you see yourself as a mother without a partner, as the world calls it a 'single mother' and are experiencing a broken or dysfunctional family, it gets much more adventurous and double the effort. It requires all your full potential to supply the emotional needs both for yourself and primarily to your lovely children.

I like to call 'single mothers' as 'full mothers', because it's required to be emotionally, physically and psychologically skilled and prepared. It requires lots of maturity, because being a full mother is one of the most inspirational and courageous challenges that can exist in the world. It is a purpose with one of the biggest responsibilities in life.

In my journey through my separation experience, I encountered different kinds of mothers, with different knowledge and skills and all must be respected, because each one of them are on a different level of spiritual growth on their own path.

I believe that we are who we choose to be. Nobody's going to come and save you, you've got to save yourself. Nobody's going to give you anything, you've got to go out and fight for it but receiving a supportive hand from community can make a huge difference when it comes to living in survival mode. Nobody knows what you want except you and nobody will be as sorry for you if you don't get it. Don't give up on your dreams!

I was incredibly surprised and happily shocked with so many people that I was meeting when I was living in the women's refuge in Lane Cove the first time I had to leave home. I have encountered so many earth angels in my life. Angels come from heaven to earth as a stranger and actually they are walking around us, every day. You just need to open your heart and see that your neighbour could be the angel that is missing in your life. I have friends that I'm so grateful for today.

Without friends and without their love, I wouldn't have coped with the situation as well as I did.

In this world, the women who I loved and admired for their strength and grace did not get that way because bad things work out. They got there because things went wrong and they handled it. They handled it in a thousand different ways, on a thousand different days, but they handled it. Those women are my super heroes and will always be.

Significant cultural change is required and I believe that we must start in the schools with programs to educate boys and girls.

The government cannot keep working as a fire brigade, just handling and trying to control the fire. We need to work on the cause and to do that we must start with the children. Children who experience abusive relationships in their families, will likely to be abusers in the future (if boys) and abused (if girls) if they do not get acknowledgement and do not get their emotions worked out and well developed.

They will accept abuse as 'normal' and will not respect themselves. There is nothing normal about being abused or about being the abuser. Healthy relationships start at home from childhood; they start from parents as role models, to teach the kids how to relate with other adults when they grow up.

I believe that if we build a campaign for primary and high schools, we can reach the kids from an early age and help them to relate with others in a respectful manner and managing frustrations in a healthier way, developing their skills and helping them to build emotional intelligence. A program that will teach them about boundaries, respect and communication skills. Teach them how to turn their crisis or their issues into opportunities of growth. Show them how to see the good thing that will be behind any problem that they encounter.

Michaela Cash, minister for employment and minister for women in Australia, says that from a policy perspective we must invest in services, progress and tools to keep women safe. We must also address the root cause of domestic violence against women, gender inequality and a lack of respect. The woman's safety package, which she recently unveiled with Prime Minister Turnbull, includes specific provisions to address this root cause. These include providing parents, teachers and students with the resources to change young people's attitudes towards violence. Investing in teaching the next generation about respectful relationships is vital if cultural change is to be realised. No Australian community is exempt from the terrible reality of domestic, family and sexual violence. We all need to be part of the solution and involved in fostering a cultural humane sense. As has been said, the standard you walk past is the standard you accept.

In this chapter I'd like to share how to stay safe after separation. When you leave the relationship, there are some steps that you need to be aware of.

For some women leaving can mean they risk losing their family and community support networks, financial security, homes, hopes and dreams. Each time a woman finds that they become stronger, clearer and more confident. The number of barriers facing a woman leaving violence may seem overwhelming, but it's important to remember that many women leave violent relationships and find safe and fulfilling lives for themselves and their children.

Women leave a violent relationship to become safe, however it is important to remember that this safety may not occur immediately. Separation can be the time of the greatest danger. It is important to have a clear safety plan for you and your children before you leave.

What to take when you leave

As a bonus with this book, I will include a safety plan with the list of the things you need to check and be aware of before leaving your home.

Before you decide to leave, you need to be in touch with your community services. This is the only way to feel safe and protected. Contact a domestic violence hotline and arrange safe accommodation for you and your children. Contact the RSPCA to arrange safe accommodation for your pets. Seek support from a domestic violence worker and consider getting an ADVO. Arrange your transportation in advance, practise travelling to your intended safe spot, prepare and safely store a living package with money, documents, clothes, and spare keys. Seek legal advice. Program emergency support services and contacts into your phone, and ask your doctor to document any injuries. Only tell trusted people of your intended relocation.

While I was living in the women's refuge in Lane Cove with my daughter and trying to keep her routine as predictable as possible with healthy people around her, I was receiving help from my social caseworker and doing art therapy and trying to express my feelings through drawing, through writing and through speaking. One of the things I was learning was that after some time from leaving the relationship, it's normal for a woman to feel the urgency to return to the relationship, and that is considered the most dangerous phase of the recovery process, like a drug addict. That's pretty sad but it happened to me too.

In the chapter *Touched by Faith* I will share how and why I decided to give trust and give it another chance for our family, leaving behind all of what I had already achieved with so much work and effort.

After leaving a controlling abusive relationship there may be moments of regret and thoughts of reuniting. These thoughts are a natural part of the grief process when dealing with the loss of a relationship. It is important to acknowledge these feelings. There are many strategies, which may be used by the abuser to encourage you to return. They may include purchasing gifts with promises of continued generosity and a better future, promise of change, saying they are sorry and that the abuse will never happen again. Use of emotional blackmail, attempts to make you feel guilty or unable to survive without them. Threats to self harm or harm you or your children or your property, harassing or intimidating visits, phone calls and text messages.

The strategies used will vary for each relationship and there are ways in which you can deal with them, including, acknowledging that the abuser's behaviour is an extension of his need to control and abuse you. Seek support through professional counselling, attend a domestic violence support group, build a strong social network, get legal advice and/or take out an Apprehended Domestic Violence Order.

This is an important time to stay connected to local support service. As a part of staying safe during the separation or even before you leave, there are some key points to remember.

Technology strategies

- ✓ Carry your mobile phone, charged, and switched on, at all times. Be confident about how to call emergency services from your handset.

- ✓ Program your mobile with all your emergency numbers (police, trusted friends and family members). Memorize emergency phone numbers in case you need to use a payphone or neighbours phone.

- ✓ If he starts abusive text messages, save text messages. Police can use these as evidence.

- ✓ Make sure that the passwords to your phone, email and bank accounts remain secret. Make sure that they are things that cannot be worked out. If you are emailing friends and family log off if you are leaving the computer unattended. This is a good habit to get into.

Financial Safety planning

- ✓ Cancel any shared credit cards, and open a new account at a different bank and keep the card at a friend's home and have bank statements delivered to a friend's home.

- ✓ If you are working, make sure your work is aware of your situation. Make sure that your wages go into your own bank account.

- ✓ Have a look at the information provided on relationship debt provided from the office of fair trading and legal aid. Keep this information at a friend's house where you will continue to have access if required.

Safety planning to protect yourself inside the home

- ✓ Identify things that have worked in the past to keep you safe.

- ✓ Think about what has happened in the past and how the abuser has acted. Identify clues that indicate when things are about to get violent (i.e. holidays, body language, drinking). Remember that perpetrators of violence are not always predictable and that it is not always possible to predict when an event is going to occur.

- ✓ If a violent incident occurs or you are worried that it might, leave if you can. DO not wait until things have gotten out of control before you leave.

- ✓ If you are ever concerned that an incident may occur, keep away from rooms with weapons (such as the kitchen) and rooms with no exits (such as the bathroom).

- ✓ Know the easiest escape routes within the home – doors, windows etc. and teach your children these routes.

- ✓ Think about where you would go if you needed to escape and who you would call. Make a plan and practice it.

- ✓ Ask your neighbours to call the police if they are worried about your safety. Make sure you know your new neighbours. Keep in mind that where you were previously you knew all your neighbours and a number of them were aware of the situation. It would be good to get to know your new neighbours to reduce the risk of losing the old neighbours who were a protective factor.

- ✓ Pack a bag with important things that you would need if you had to leave your home quickly, leave it in a safe place or with a friend or relative you trust. Include cash, a spare set of keys, some clothing for you and your children, as well as important documents including court papers, copy of your Apprehended Domestic Violence Order, passports, birth certificates medical records (inc. children's 'blue books') medical records and medicines.

Support strategies

- ✓ Inform your neighbours that there is a history of violence. Ask them to call the police if they hear a disturbance at your home.

- ✓ Attend a support group with women who have had similar experiences. Keep in contact with your support services such as Angela.

- ✓ Arrange a password with your family or friends. In the event of an emergency, where it is not safe for you to call the police directly, you may be able to call a friend without attracting attention. Use the password to let them know that you are unsafe and that they should call the police.

- ✓ Keep your DV related information, particularly information with details of support services including yours at a friend's home.

- ✓ Keep a copy of your old ADVO at the house in a place that you can get it if you need to provide it to the police. Keep in mind that it is common for perpetrators of violence to encourage women to throw away old documents or remove these documents without the woman's knowledge.

Legal strategies

- ✓ Always call the police if there is a breach of your Apprehended Domestic Violence Order or if you don't have one to arrange assistance if there has been violence. Make sure that they are aware of the history.

- ✓ Keep a diary of any abuse. Record anything that made you feel uncomfortable or unsafe. Write down the substance of any conversation, and any threatening or intimidating statements. This will be very helpful if you have to go to court.

- ✓ Keep a copy of your ADVO with you e.g. in your handbag, at home, at work or with a trusted friend.

Online Safety Strategies

- ✓ If you have been sharing a computer with the offender, be aware that both sent and received emails can be accessed along with a history of websites that you have visited. Empty your deleted items folder and your CACHE (the place where your computer stores all the information you have browsed) regularly so these cannot be accessed

- ✓ If you feel at all unsure that your computer is not a 'safe zone', then wherever possible use a friends computer, an internet café or the internet facility at your local library (often, a staff member at a library would be able to teach you how to empty your deleted items and your CACHE if your unsure)

To make it easier for you, this list is also printed in the appendices of this book for ready reference.

If you want to help a friend

If you have a friend and you have the feeling they're being abused, you can help her in many ways following these steps:

1. Set up a time to talk. Try to make sure you have privacy and won't be distracted or interrupted. Let a friend know you are concerned about her safety and be supportive. Listen to your friend. Keep in mind that it might be very hard for her to talk about her abuse. Offer specific help. You might say you are willing to just listen, help her with childcare or to provide transportation, for example. Don't place shame, blame or guilt on your friend. Don't say 'you just need to leave'. Instead, just say something like, 'I get scared thinking about what might happen to you.' Tell her you understand that her situation is very difficult.

2. Help her make a safety plan. Safety plan includes picking a place to go and packing important items. Encourage a friend to talk to someone who can help.

3. Offer to help her find a local or domestic violence agency. Offer to go with her to the agency, the police or court. If your friend decides to stay, continue to be supportive. Your friend may decide to stay in the relationship or she may leave and then go back many times. It may be hard for you to understand, but people who stay in abusive relationships do so for many reasons, be supportive, no matter what your friend decides to do.

4. Encourage your friend to do things outside the relationship. It's important for her to see friends and family. If your friend decides to leave, continue to offer support, even if she thought the relationship was abusive, she may feel sad or lonely, once it's over. Perhaps she needs help getting services from agencies or community groups. Keep in mind that you can't rescue your friend. She has to be the one to decide it's time to get help, support her no matter what her decision. Let your friend know that you'll always be there no matter what.

When you get connected to the community and services you will feel safer and you will be stronger to make decisions about the future of your family. Let yourself be touched by the community. Be open and be humble, because if you are open, things will come to you when you least expect. Miracles can happen in your life, you just need to believe it. The person you become after all the things you go through will be much more experienced and wiser. Engage with the community. Be part of the courses, the workshops, read good books and talk to people who have experience and have much to teach you. You will be able to build knowledge to have a new vision for your future.

During my experience while I was dealing with this strange new world, outside my home and feeling vulnerable, and with my little daughter under my wing to provide and to be protected, I was building an incredible network with so many organisations. I can't thank enough a number of friends, The Salvation Army, Saint Vincent De Paul, and many others acknowledged in this book. Also at the end of this book you will find a resource list of how and where to get support.

Chapter 8

Touched by Growth

'The tiny seed knew that in order to grow, it needed to be dropped in dirt, covered with darkness, and struggle to reach the light.'

– Wayne Dyer

What you get by achieving your goals is not as important as what you become by achieving your goals. The world is full of blessings and opportunities. Many people have big dreams, but few actually fulfil their potential. It is rare for someone to truly live out the dreams that they once had for themselves. What is the one thing you were put on this earth to achieve?

Find out what that is for you and how you can make it happen. Your time on earth is limited to about 85 years, 31,000 days, 744,000 hours, 44,640,000 minutes. How we live each minute will bring the next. Starting a new project in life is like throwing yourself off the cliff and assembling an airplane on the way down. Our big goal is how we are going to spend this one and precious life and opportunity we have been given. Are you going to spend it trying to look good and creating the illusion that you have the power or the circumstance, or whether you're going to taste it, enjoy it and find out the truth about who you really are?

It's not about whom you will spend your life with. Your soul mate is often not someone who comes into your life peacefully. It is the person who comes to make you question things, who changes your reality, somebody that marks a before and after in your life.

I found my inner peace. It was not through material gain. Your inner peace is not in your house, or friends, or cars or even religion. It's not in your job. Your inner peace can be found in accepting and loving ourselves for who God made us to be. Your inner peace is in your dignity and self-respect.

It is in your confidence and knowing that you can achieve anything you put your mind to. The power is within us; the light to shine is within us. If we awaken our inner light, we are actually connecting with our truth. The truth of what we are supposed to be, to grow to be as full as we are destined to be in this journey of experience and growth, called life.

Victims spend their time pointing to their problems; winners spend their time looking for solutions. One thing is for certain, if you don't try, you can't fail, but nor can you succeed. Courage is not the absence of fear; it is the willingness to act despite the fear. In the middle of difficulty lies the opportunity and as a consequence, the growth.

Since 2011, I have been participating and engaging in courses, workshops, webinars, groups, books, and reading where I have been developing my skills to be able to improve myself as a person and as a soul. Some friends who are going through difficulties in their life and relationships have asked for my help and I have been able to give them some guidance to help them to make better decision in their lives. I was really touched by growth and touched by growth means that I have been growing a lot.

Just as being a mother was the biggest step in my life that turned me into a better person, I am always hoping to learn more about everything. I love books, I love information, I love to hear about people's experience and I really like to get to know about people's behaviours.

I have studied extensively about intimacy and caring communication skills, the toxic attraction between an empath and a narcissist, causes and consequences of domestic violence and abusive relationships. Also courses about the difference between healthy and unhealthy relationships, how domestic violence affects kids and much more.

All of this study has helped me to grow as a person to be prepared for different situations that I wouldn't have been prepared for before. I have been asked by friends about becoming a social worker. 'Why don't you use your experience and knowledge to support women in situations that you have lived before?' I think that working this closely with people would be hard for me as I am very sensitive and I would get too involved with their situations because I am an empath.

Self-education is one of the most important acts that you can have to develop your skills and rebuild yourself, personally and spiritually. When we are in a crisis we need to dig deep into ourselves so that we can rise to a new level of strength. Self-education is how you do that, because you can find out how to use you own innate strength in a better way in order to get through.

No one is immune to adversity and yet it's human nature that you don't give much thought to your ability to cope with a serious problem until you are actually faced with a crisis. Even so, the people who are far more likely to emerge from the experience far more confident emotionally are those who focus on opportunities for growth. One thing is certain, the pain you feel today is the strength you feel tomorrow. For every challenge encountered there is an opportunity to grow and of course blessings to be seen. Growth is one of the biggest blessings you can find in a crisis situation.

How I found the blessing of growth through a crisis

While living in a women's refuge, I was exposed to a number of learning opportunities through art therapy, specialised DV counselling, workshops, organisations meetings, which gave me the opportunity to dig deep into my sub-conscious, understanding the reasons of many different feelings. Facing reality is the key of changing because denying or minimising the circumstances for our situation or trying to avoid the pain we are feeling, only postpones having to confront the new life ahead. Suppressed feelings never really fade away, they just remain in the shadows until the next time you are faced with a problem or loss and then they resurface stronger and more painful than ever. The only way you can get to the other side of your pain is to push through it by accepting the reality of your circumstance and giving yourself permission to express the hurt, the anger and the pain you are feeling in a healthy way.

There may be decisions that can't wait and spending some time coming to terms with the reality of your circumstance, assessing your options and gut feelings and taking small steps forward will help regain some feelings of stability and control in our life. Reaching out by talking to someone can help to relieve the burden and provide assurance that you are not alone. Sometimes it's just a matter of having somebody listen. Other times it helps to have a different perspective on how to navigate through the healing process. People will appear in your life from nowhere and you'll be surprised how many people you'll get to know through your crisis situation and they are here at that time to help you in a better way, because the universe is helping you to be rewarded because of the hard decision you have made.

After studying and researching for the past five years, since my first traumatic separation, and with the desire to save and protect my sanity against emotionally breaking down, I had the opportunity to improve my knowledge through personal development attending numerous courses, workshops and webinars; art therapy, counselling, parenting skills, childhood intrinsic memory, meditation, mindfulness, and everything related to get to know more about myself and about healthy/unhealthy relationships, abusive relationships, controlling and narcissist behaviour and domestic violence issues. Now I am able to understand much better where I stand and from where a person's subconscious behaviour is coming from.

One of the things that really helped me a lot was volunteering. It's amazing how helping someone else who's going through crisis can put your own situation into a different, more positive light. Avoid self-blame, because self-blame is an insidious emotion that can quickly overwhelm you, especially when dealing with crisis.

It's human nature to feel that somehow you should have known or been able to prevent a situation. Don't waste time worrying about what you could, should, and would have done differently. Just because you have hit a few rough spots on your journey doesn't mean your future can't be better than you ever imagined.

Moving forward with your life, or deciding to linger and suffer, is a choice only you can make. Look for the lessons. There is a lesson in every moment of your life. I believe that nothing is coincidence and everything that comes to you comes for a reason. One of the biggest matters for me to be touched by growth is to always look for the lessons. As tough as life's lessons sometimes are, each holds the opportunity for growth and to reach a better understanding about who we are and what matters most for us. Choosing to ignore these lessons may well mean we find ourselves facing the same opportunity again and again.

Have you ever known someone who has the same bad experience repeated over and over again? As getting into car accidents, been laid off many times or have had multiple marriages? When the same thing happens over and over again, then it's time to start looking deeper for the root cause to improve your situation. You may not feel like it, but it's important to maintain as much of your routine and regular schedule as possible. This means getting plenty of sleep each night and eating a balanced diet.

Try spending some time each day simply relaxing or focusing on your breathing and you'll see a positive difference in the state of your mind and the amount of tension you hold in your body. Learn to trust again. The harsh reality is that we are often blindsided from what seems like the safest places. A relationship you thought was strong is destroyed by betrayal, a friendship suddenly gone with no explanation; a job you invested your whole heart in has been taken from you in a flash.

Being blindsided by a crisis can leave you feeling insecure and vulnerable. Learning to trust again may be the most difficult part of recovering from a crisis, because we'll do almost everything to keep experiencing the pain again. To put yourself out in the world is risky. But the world needs your gifts and your love and if you close yourself off, you'll be wasting a very precious life.

It's impossible to avoid getting hurt from time to time, but the reward for taking the risk is a well-lived life. Remember, we are always near our hope. We are all capable of more and that's why we are here, growing in this world. One of the things for sure that's going to happen to you is that you will become a better person. It doesn't matter if you want to or not, because growth is the natural consequence of a crisis situation. You must be facing resilience and you must be strong enough to find ideas to get out of the crisis. In that process you'll experience growth whether you want to or not. We create heartbreak and disappointment when insisting that specific people behave in specific ways and when attached to unimportant details. I was reading an interesting article about having success in life and the big question wasn't what you want to enjoy, but instead, what pain do you want to sustain. The quality of life is determined by the quality of dealing and coping with your negative experiences, which will drive you to get to know how you can cope with your life and deal with people. There is no such thing as a pain free life and how we choose to suffer will determine the quality of our lifelong journey.

Life is a process of choices and as a consequence, growth. If we are not enjoying the process to achieve something, it's probably unlikely we can achieve the goal. We want the result, but are not willing to struggle to achieve the process and the result.

Understanding requires compassion, patience and a willingness to believe that good hearts sometimes choose full methods. Through judging we separate, through understanding we grow. Through the process of growth you can start to help others, once you are safe, secure and successful in your own life. Practically every successful person you know of is successful in part because they move the destructive and disruptive people out of their life. Successful people carefully manage their energy and associations. They are gatekeepers. Limiting their exposure to healthy and supportive people, love themselves enough to say no to people who diminish their chances for a beautiful and empowered life.

Sometimes you have to get away from what you know to discover what you don't know. When you feel that it's time for the abuse, control, lies and negativity to end, that's when you are growing yourself and your inner light will be shining very brightly.

Connect to people who are living the positive lifestyle you wish for yourself and who share your values and create a new family or friends that you can call home. Your new positive and supportive tribe will empower you to serve others in ways you would have never before imagined, to be able to take care of others, you must start to take care of yourself, so then you're going to be powerful to help others.

Any time that a person withdraws from something that is challenging them, that may be the very thing that they are meant to grow through. Running from challenge is not usually the wisest answer, it's usually wise to tackle the challenge and take advantage of an opportunity to make a difference.

A workshop I once participated in was about the metaphor of the shark cage. The metaphor and the principles are simple. The elements of the shark cage metaphor are the shark, the dolphin, the fish, the cage barriers and the treasure box. The shark represents the abuser in the unhealthy relationship. The shark character is being controlling, selfish, narcissist, blaming, playing mind games, being sneaky, charismatic, unpredictable, unbalanced, unhappy, weak, greedy, vengeful, abusive, isolating, playing victim, disrespectful, fearful, intimidating, and arrogant.

The dolphin represents the healthy relationship. What are the characteristics of a healthy person in a relationship? Integrity, accountability, peace, love, consideration, compassion, harmony, joy, forgiving, teamwork, active listener, self care, self love, support, community, protective, responsible, communication, selfless, loyal, trustworthy, shares feelings, respect, awareness, has empathy. The partner of the collared victim (a word that I don't like because for me we are survivors, not victims) is the fish.

Who are you? Which kind of fish are you? What characteristics do you have? In my case I'm an empathetic person, I have compassion and I'm very spiritual. I like communication, I'm a forgiving person, capable, reliable, and trustful, I have honour. Draw your characteristics in a fish. The cage bars will represent where your weaknesses are. Each bar can represent where you must strengthen your protection and boundaries. See the picture on the appendices.

Think of each bar and what they might represent. For me, on one of the bars I wrote, I have a right to express my opinions and feelings, I have the right to say no, if it doesn't feel right to me, I have a right to be treated with respect, I have a right to my personal space, I have the right to change my mind, I have the right to be free of abuse, I have a right to be heard, I have a right to have fun.

Finally the treasure box is everything that makes you feel good, empowers you and makes you feel happy. In my treasure box I would say things like: healthy eating, self development, reading good books, spiritual movies, yoga, travelling, nature, massage, music, counselling, comedy, quality time with friends. Most important for me in my treasure box is to create opportunities and experience with a quality life with my daughter. Walking on the beach, dancing, laughing, and having fun. In your growth path as your consciousness, refinement and pureness of heart expands, you will become less judgmental. Less corrective, less reactive, less black and white, less critical, less apt to blame and less tormented by others and their faults and views.

That's a big part of your growth. Boundaries and assertiveness were another level of development that I was going through during my growth journey. What are boundaries? A boundary is a limit or an edge that defines you as separate from others. It's a limit that promotes integrity or a sense of wholeness. We have other boundaries like emotional, spiritual, sexual and relational. Clear boundaries feel good, they are flexible enough that we can choose what to let in and what to keep out and we can determine to exclude meanness and hostility and let in affection, kindness, positivity, regard and respect.

There are some myths that are important for us to be aware of. They are not true. For example, you have to be polite to everyone. You have to think of others before yourself. If you put yourself first you are selfish. Girls are not allowed to get angry and boys not allowed to cry. It's more important to ignore your feelings than get into conflict. This is the most important thing: that your love is unconditional and their needs come before yours. Thinking is more important than feeling. Words do not hurt. Domestic violence is only physical. If a woman is upset she is automatically premenstrual. If you are a strong, independent woman able to air your own knowledge about worldly events and who is not in a relationship, your sexuality can be questioned. Child rearing is solely the job for the female. If a woman has a family she must give up her career.

Those untrue statements must be out of your life. Women can pretend, deny, wear a mask and allow themselves to become manipulated by a set of belief systems. Are we able to free ourselves from these myths? From this chapter about *touched by growth*, if you can have two things that will help you be your whole self, it can be like that. There are two kinds of selves. The pseudo self and the real self.

Sometimes we can put on a mask when we present ourselves to the world and that is the pseudo self. The pseudo self can take on or include agreeing with others in order to be liked, inability to accept compliments, avoiding conflict, feelings of jealousy, independent of others and may not enjoy their own company. Being assertive in all or most situations. If you get stuck in your pseudo self and continue to allow your pseudo self to have control of you, people can become stuck and not realise their full potential.

The real self is the real unique self that each person was born to be. There are different names for this, but the real self can include being in charge of our own thoughts and knowing the difference between thoughts and feelings. Having self-confidence in beliefs and conditions. We say, what do I think as opposed to what do other people think? Can give and receive compliments, has integrity and is honest and stays true to their innermost values and is confident and assertive.

Don't forget that the process of growth is a work in progress and never stops. When you see yourself in a big process of growth being blessed, you will be blessed with loving yourself more, respecting your boundaries, responding instead of reacting, understand boundary breakers, boundary violations, lower anxiety, stop people pleasing and deal better with conflict.

The blessings of growth can be a big list and would just depend on your self and your efforts. As part of the growth process, you have to have the willingness to take risks, initially in low risk situations and then as our confidence and skills increase in more scary situations.

A willingness to value yourself as well as other people, a willingness to accept the fact that you won't always get what you want, a willingness to accept the fact that there is no such thing as a perfect response to every situation. A willingness to be open to new ways and handle new situations, a willingness to accept goals, a willingness that not everyone will like you and be able to accept the fact, a willingness to desire fairness and do all you can to achieve it with accepting that sometimes fairness does not always occur and the willingness to accept that acquiring new skills requires effort and practice. We are the only one who controls our thoughts and we are the only one who can make a decision for growth through believing that there are blessings behind the crisis situation.

Remember we cannot evolve unless we are willing to change. We will never better ourselves, if we always cling to what was.

> *'The past is where you learned the lesson.*
> *The future is where you apply the lesson.'*
>
> – Luciane Sperling

The Relationship Spectrum

Relationships can range from healthy to abusive, and some relationships may be unhealthy, but not abusive. Here's a breakdown of the relationship spectrum:

A Healthy Relationship	An Unhealthy Relationship	An Abusive Relationship
A healthy relationship means that both you and your partner are...	An unhealthy relationship starts when just one of you...	An abusive relationship starts when just one of you...
1) **Communicating** You talk openly about problems without shouting or yelling. You listen to one another, hear each other out, respect each other's opinions, and are willing to compromise.	1) **Not Communicating** Problems are not talked about at all. You don't listen to each other or try to compromise.	1) **Communicates abusively** During disagreements there is screaming, cursing, or threatening, or these things happen even when there is no argument. A partner is demeaning or insulting towards the other.
2) **Respectful** You value each other as you are. Culture, beliefs, opinions and boundaries are valued. You treat each other in a way that demonstrates the high esteem you hold for one another.	2) **Disrespectful** One or both partners are inconsiderate towards the other. One or both partners don't treat each other in a way that shows they care.	2) **Is disrespectful through abuse** A partner intentionally and continuously disregards your feelings and physical safety.
3) **Trusting** You both trust each other, and the trust has been earned.	3) **No trusting** There is suspicion that your partner is doing things behind your back, or your partner is suspicious of your loyalty without any reason.	3) **Falsely accuses the other of flirting or cheating** A partner suspects flirting or cheating without reason and accuses the other, often harming their partner verbally or physically as a results.
4) **Hones** You are both honest with each other but can still choose to keep certain things private. For example, you both know that it is important to be honest about things that affect or involve the relationship and still know that it is also o.k. to keep certain things private.	4) **Dishonest** One or both partners are telling lies to each other.	4) **Doesn't take responsibility for the abuse** The violent or verbally abusive partner denies or minimizes their actions. They try to blame the other for the harm they're doing.
5) **Equal** You make decisions together and you hold each other to the same standards.	5) **Trying to take control** One or both partners sees their desires or decisions as more important. One partner is or both partners are focused only on getting their own way.	5) **Controls the other partner** There is no equality in the relationship. What one partner says goes, and if the other partner tries to change this there is increased abuse.
6) **Enjoy Personal Space** You both enjoy spending time apart and respect when one of your voices a need for space.	6) **Feeling smothered or forgetting to spend time with others** So much time is spent together that one partner is beginning to feel uncomfortable. Or sometimes both partners spend so much time together that they ignore friends, family or other things that used to be important to them.	6) **Isolates the other partner** One partner controls where the other one goes, who the other partner sees and talk to. The other partner has no personal space and is often isolated from other people altogether.

Chapter 9
Touched by Faith

'Faith gives us strength to reach beyond our ability and trust sustains us on the journey.'

– Ken Duncan

Whether you are experiencing a relationship breakdown or other life challenges, they can be difficult to manage if you don't know how to internally process what you are experiencing. It is wise to find and focus on the blessings. By taking the time to look for the blessings, you give yourself the edge to dealing with the challenges that you encounter. One of my main characteristics and gifts is that I have big faith in the biggest energy of this universe and I believe that everything I need will come to me when I need it, and it doesn't matter what belongs to me, it's trying already to find a way to meet me and be part of my life. Having faith is to know in your heart that what you hope for will actually happen, assuring you to believe things that cannot be seen.

One of the good questions to ask yourself is how can you give others what they would love, while simultaneously receiving what you would love? Entering into a relationship with God is the greatest exchange in the world. We give everything that we have, broken hearts for example, and he gives us everything that we need. We are a mess without Him. Your worst day with God will be better than your best day without him and when I say God, you can call it anything that you want, but believe that there is a higher power in this universe that is really driving your life for the best that can happen to you. The highest power above us can restore the power if you're willing to turn away from your mistakes.

When we invite Jesus to come into our hearts we become the home of God. He lives in us. You never have to solve problem again, because if you believe and you have faith, you know that He promises that He will never leave us. My faith helped me always; because having faith means that I always have hope, strength, determination, because the greater one lives in me. Love is always the final and most complete cure to our inner demons.

When you realise that your life is just a story of you in this world, you can feel more content. That is, your life is no longer more problematic, because it's just a story of you. It's not your identity, it's just a story of you and you can change a story any time you desire. The transformational consciousness happens when you are aware of the now, itself, beyond the phenomena that arises in your life and you start to live no longer in a reaction, but you will be based in facts and will respond in peace.

I was blessed enough to be found by a friend I will be deeply grateful forever. He was like an angel in the form of a human being with a big heart. He has a higher level of spirituality based on universal love and knowledge about human behaviour based on forgiveness. He was my spiritual and emotional rescuer for the time I was living in Lane Cove. He was responsible for keeping me going when I was doing it tough, by listening, bringing God's words, looking after me and Joahnne without asking or expecting anything in return. He would come expectantly to my home bringing shopping, nappies, remedies and weekly making sure we were fine. He would secretly fill my car with petrol and return the car back, with me noticing it just later on. He would guide me with wise advice when I was freaking out. He had always an honoured and respectful attitude. He understood my pain between the 'love' and the 'hate' feeling about my husband. I was feeling safe and deeply blessed for being worthy of having this 'human angel' around. Though wary, he also helped me to make the decision about reuniting with my husband, as he said everyone can have a second chance to make it right, if showing authentic repentance and willing to make it right through better choices.

After not seeing each other for months because Joahnne and I were under Apprehended Domestic Violence Order protection since we left home, and because he made the mistake in court twice while denying the ADVO to the magistrate, he again was allowed to have contact with Joahnne, after we had mediation with a lawyer that was allocated by my social worker to Joahnne. The visits were supposed to be supervised by me. That was emotionally very difficult requiring lots of strength.

At one of the visits at Dee Why beach, he put together all his strength to say *sorry*, and how he didn't want to be like that and how much he wished to have his family back. I saw a broken man, hurt, repentant and humble. I didn't like that he was saying that in front of Joahnne in the car before going back to our home in Lane Cove, but I saw in his eyes the man I married one day. I wasn't expecting that and being caught on the touching moment I felt confused and tried to avoid the conversation, leaving quickly with my heart pumping with anxiety and feeling all the emotional mess rising in my head touching my deep desires. I saw both having inside so much unspoken pain and unspoken love to be addressed. Over the following days, slowly, we were having more contact and the contact was giving me a sense of pleasure and happiness, but uncertainty. I don't know how I allowed myself to be hooked back in a such short time, as his last very mean email was sent out just August and by December I was back home in Dee Why. Of course I was a little bit fearful that it wouldn't work, I was giving over all my trust when he said that he was willing to make a go of it giving to our little family a chance to use the experience and try to build a different end story for the future. I had some friends being reluctant about it and my family wasn't very happy, but they also had the hope that he too can change. His family were much more excited about it, as they knew some of the mistakes he had made. I always showed love and respect to his parents and siblings, I never mixed what he was doing in our relationship with his family. Luckily I have been receiving back from them the fair and respectful treatment, and more, as his parents show honest affection towards me.

How did the second chance happen?

It was based in hope, faith and believing in his authentic repentance, that at the end of 2011, I decided to give our relationship another go, exposing my heart again. Nothing would haunt me more in the future than the regret of not giving it a go. I didn't know how exactly I was going to forget all the name callings that were still in my head, the horrible emails, the mistreatments in the past, plus forget that he had sex with another women while we were experiencing those moments of crisis. I didn't know how to face my friends and everyone who helped me through this process, and didn't know how to announce that decision to my family. But I was going to figure out how to manage all of that and I knew that my 'bar' now was higher, so I knew that I wouldn't accept any type of abuse anymore, he was meeting a new women, would he be able to handle it? Because I wanted to assure myself and avoid exposing Joahnne to something that would force us to leave again, I needed to make sure things would really have the best chance for success. I knew that we needed support from professionals and we couldn't do it by ourselves, so he was happy to agree and follow the safe plan my social worker made for us. He was supposed to enrol in a course at Relationships Australia and get couple counselling sessions. The course was called "Taking Responsibility, a course for men who want to take responsibility for their behaviour patterns in intimate relationships". This course supports men to take responsibility for their actions and to realise alternative ways of relating and managing their behaviour. It also helps strengthen attitudes and skills necessary for respectful, fair and loving relationships with female partners and children.

He was also surprisingly going to the 'church' with me and Joahnne, and was reading the Gospel with me, so it looked like we were bonding again, he was communicating again, listening, caring about my feelings, so I decided to give up all that I had already achieved for me and Joahnne and I moved back to Dee Why to live again in the unit we were renting for more than two years before I left. I really wanted it to work, I wanted my family together, I wanted to be with my husband, I wanted my daughter to be raised with her mum and dad in a healthy relationship, I wanted to get older together, and I was dreaming about the future where we would be watching back and saying, 'Yes, we lived all that period of serious crisis but we are here healed and together, we are winners and we loved each other so much that we were able to get all the help possible and use it to save our family'. I didn't want to give up the 'good memories', the 'good part of what we had one day' I wanted to feel that again, I wanted to see again the man I married. The worst grief you can have is the grief of something that is still alive inside your heart, even if deeply hidden inside. I saw him trying his best to impress me again, within his limited mature emotional capabilities, and I believed that if possible, the painful consequences he went through during our past events would be enough to avoid the same mistakes in the future. My faith was based on the possibility of freeing himself from demand of ego and be true and humble in his love, improve communications skills, that he would work in his past family issues based on a negative relationship role model he learnt from his parents, and so then he would finally see and use his higher self to make decisions about future emotional traps towards us as couple and protect his most precious treasure: his family. I was also willing to commit myself to address my own emotional traps that would damage future efforts of connection and have courage to speak out to him and bring awareness if old behaviour would occur, instead of being mistakenly quiet and frightened as I was in the past. I wouldn't reunite if I believed I was going 'back' to what we had. I believed we were reuniting but going 'forward' to a 'new' relationship. A sign of the 'old' relationship with any abusive behaviour wasn't going to be accepted anymore and I would stick seriously on that point. The good is that now I was well informed and much more mature about those signs that could occur while reuniting and I also knew where to get help if the cycle of abuse was going to escalate. In my belief, one year would show things progressing or walking backwards.

Unfortunately after less than three months I was watching him giving up each one of his promises and engaged activities. He wasn't happy to go to the course any more, was complaining, and saying that the course wasn't really for him. I was feeling betrayed, trapped, and with deep disappointment my hope started to shrink. I knew that I was doing my part but also I knew that if he would stop doing his part, the plan would fail and so our relationship would fail too, forever.

I assumed all the risks about returning home because of my family values and real love. I did it with hope, for pure love with all my faith. And I knew that if I didn't have a try, I would never know if that would work or not. At some point I saw myself doing therapy to learn how to deal with a person that was supposed to be doing therapy. Unfortunately subconscious was taking over his behaviour and I was seeing the return of some old habits, covering his love, but at this time it was much more subtle than before although the list of categories was getting clearly present. I was now identifying the signs easier due to the knowledge I had received. Things like silent threatening, avoiding and rejection, hot and cold attitude, denial, undermining, criticizing, ordering, threatening, sarcasm and hostility were – finding space again. He was again going out, isolating himself from us and drinking more. I was not only disappointed, but in fear and feeling hopeless about seeing him defeating himself, but still giving time, observing and waiting. When I realised that the damage was getting bigger and not getting better, I sadly and hopeless began to think about the next step.

Just because someone isn't clear about their own feelings doesn't give them the right to screw with someone else's feelings. I wasn't sure if he was able to see the sorrow behind my smile, the love behind his anger and the reason behind my silence.

I got to a point where the hardest decision was to walk away again or try even harder, but how much more would I lose myself trying harder alone? In my process of hope I was recreating myself, the new me. I realised how much 'love' must be respected and so because I love my daughter and had learned again how to love my worth, and myself, I was empowered to respect my feelings and instincts. Faith is all about believing, you may not know how it will happen, but you know it will.

Is it likely to change? Men's use of violent and controlling behaviour rarely just stops. Your partner may be quite sincere when he promises it will never happen again. Unfortunately, most men find that they cannot keep such promises without support and assistance from professional services.

Participant's in a men's behaviour change group is no guarantee of change. Some men do give up controlling their partner and stop their use of abuse. Others might stop their use of physical violence but continue other forms of abuse or control. Men who attend, but do not really make an effort might not change their ways at all. Others might take a long time to change, or change for a while but slip back into their old ways from time to time.

You are the best judge of whether your partner is really willing to take action to improve his intimacy skills, or changing enough for his family sake, but you should make that judgement based on his actions, not your hopes.

Some men might have a problem with expressing angry feelings; others might be experiencing difficulties expressing feelings such as fear, anxiety or frustration. Stopping the use of controlling actions is about a lot more than managing anger. One of the facts that best highlights this is that men who use controlling behaviour towards their partner often don't use it towards anyone else. They can control their anger, but in certain settings, and with certain people, they choose not to.

When you contact the infinite soul inside yourself, you can trust in guidance. The truth, the ideas, the encouragement that you have all the information inside yourself, you just need to listen, pay attention and allow yourself to go where you believe you're worth being and more importantly where you believe is a better place to guide your inner child.

Remember that bad habits create bad thoughts; bad thoughts create bad feelings. Be careful with your thoughts. Change your thoughts, it is about decision, and you will meet better feelings. Your action will be different because you will be acting based on good feelings.

Remember that we are people of divine work. I remember looking at past events in my life and in each one of them I had this feeling of a powerful calling, a burning desire that calls me to take action and be prepared for the next step of life.

We need to listen to the message from the higher self, talking to you each day. It's your personal intelligence. Divine intelligence is inside you and you need just to connect. Make a decision and have faith in your decision. Have a life that's worth living, better than running away from problems, it's better to embrace them, take action and find solutions. What's happening with people that are acting under negative behaviour or thoughts?

Is it for sure that they're trying their best around their capability or what they consider to be their best? But what's happening is that the subconscious takes over and people return to the old habits. Our mind is powerful, but you are not driving it because you are sitting at the back, subconsciously. Be awake, awake to the next level of life, of potentiality.

Some people refuse to face their feelings because it's too hard. Remember that the voice in your head is not you. Learn to figure out when the voice is really you. Be awake to the present and exercise mindfulness. When we are truly inspired by something, we cannot fail, because we don't give up. You might fall, maybe several times, but you will always get back up again. Faith will take you places where reason will not allow you to go. We have those inner callings all the time but for some reason we decide to follow the noise, instead of the soul.

In this society people try to fit in instead of being themselves. They try to fit in to be accepted and loved and they forget about their own gift. We are here to stand out and not to fit in. We are here for the awakening and the awareness of ourselves. We are already loved and accepted by the universe and that is why we are here.

When you decide to hear your soul, that's when you can finally recognise yourself and have those 'aha' moments in life. Your life perception will switch forever. As I said before in this book, we are not a body with a soul, we are a soul with a body and our soul has destiny, purpose. The road of self-development and spiritual growth is open to everyone. But unfortunately just a few will be able to reach this point before they encounter the time when they will be called to return to their real home.

I love butterflies and their ability of transformation. When creating my business 'My Inner Light' I wanted to have my signature with a little butterfly on top. I really relate to the butterfly, because I feel like I'm transforming from a caterpillar to a beautiful and free butterfly. A butterfly is a symbol of transformation and transformation is happening in your life when you start to work on your faith and believe in yourself and respect the higher power, which drives this universe, the entire universe.

> *'When one of the caterpillars transformed into a butterfly, the other caterpillar spoke not of her beauty, but of her weirdness. They wanted her to change back into what she always had been. But the butterfly had wings and she flew.'*
>
> – Dean Jackson

One thing to remember is to be tolerant of those who are lost on their path. Ignorance, conceit, anger, jealousy and greed stem from a lost soul. Pray that they will find guidance. Have faith in yourself and don't downgrade your dream to match your reality, but yes, upgrade your faith to match your destiny. If you fail, never give up, because I learnt that FAIL, means First Attempt In Learning. And END is not the end as it means Effort Never Dies and a NO means Next Opportunity.

In the midst of tears, we can find an invincible smile for everything. With positive and invincible love, hate will never win. In the midst of chaos, we can find an invincible calm and in the midst of winter, we find us an invincible summer. No matter how hard the world pushes against me, within me will prevail something stronger, something better pushing right back, that is resilience. Remember that it doesn't matter which spiritual path, religion or doctrine you decide to follow, what's really important and whatever your faith is, it must help you to be a better person in this world.

Growing your spirituality will help you to grow as a person. I trust that everything happens for a reason, even if we are not wise enough to see it.

When there is no struggle there is no strength, so the opportunity is in the middle of the crisis and with faith you can reach everything you want in life. I believe that all experience in life is designed to shape ourselves and reform us into the ultimate and greatest version of ourselves that you could ever imagine yourself to be.

When you come to believe that a power greater than yourself could restore you to sanity, that's a big step for you for your recovery.

The big question is, how do you find hope? For me it is having faith in a higher power and knowing that my life story has a purpose.

> 'Now faith is confidence in what we hope for, an assurance about what we do not see.'
> – Hebrews 11:1.

In the path of faith, you will learn to love who you are instead of what you do. At the beginning of this year I decided to do a course called Recovery and a few days later I was reading a book called *Set Yourself Free*, by Chile Smith. She is a counsellor and motivational speaker and as the program director of recovery sources, she has developed many courses in personal development and designed programs for the treatment of co-dependency and addiction. She's originally from the United States, but Chile is now a permanent resident of Australia and is recognised as one of the country's leading specialists in this field. Reading her book I encountered exactly the same 12-step program that I was doing this year in Australia. In Chapter 12, *Touched by Recovery*, I'm going to be explaining a bit more about this program, the steps and benefits.

In order to keep working on my faith and my spirituality, I decided to be part of a church in the Central Coast, called EV Church. Since Joahnne was one year old we were always going to a spiritualist house at Dee Why Beach and since I moved to Gosford I was trying to keep working on printing God's name in her heart, so that's the best legacy that I could leave for my daughter: to have faith and believe in the higher power and be grounded. Faith is an important skill you can leave for your child, because it doesn't matter what happens in their life, they will be certain to work on their faith and receive what they need. They will feel protected, because they believe that they will be protected.

Before we finish this chapter about faith and hope, I'd like to leave you with an exercise. Would you be willing to do a spiritual catalogue of your life?

In one spiritual list you can openly examine and confess your faults or anything that you did in your life that you didn't like, but in your spiritual list you can also write about all the things that you feel proud of. Think about your mind, your body, your family, and your church. At the end of this book I'm going to give you the life evaluation worksheet, so you can work a little bit on your inventory and try to figure out your life evaluation, because if you have faith and you face your life with honesty, you know where you are and you can decide where you're going to be.

Faith can save you in many ways and when you have faith and you believe in a higher power greater than yourself that can restore you to sanity. Insanity has been described as doing the same things over and over again expecting a different result each time. Sanity has been defined as willingness of mind making decisions based on the truth.

When you believe in your higher power you receive some gifts and they are strength, acceptance, new life, integrity, trust. 1 Corinthians 10-13 says, 'And God is faithful, he will not let you be tempted beyond what you can bear, but when you are tempted he will also provide a way out.'

Remember that feelings are not facts; we need to have feelings and facts together to be able to make decisions. The decision is just in your hands. You made a decision to turn your life and your wheels over to the care of God or the higher power, whatever you want to call it.

Take action to start to work on your faith and be committed to your decision.

'If you abide in my word, you really are my disciples. And you will know the truth, and the truth will set you free'

– John 8-31

Chapter 10

Touched by Forgiveness

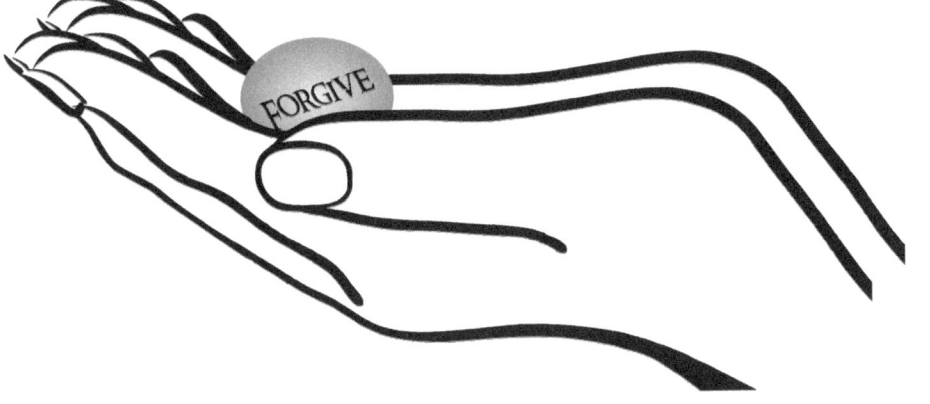

'The weak can never forgive. Forgiveness is the attribute of the strong.'

– Mahatma Gandhi

Forgiveness has nothing to do with what we feel. Forgiveness is a decision we make about how we treat the person to be forgiven. Our goal will be to learn to do what is right. Through the process of growth, we learn that we forgive people in our life, even those who are not sorry for their actions. Holding onto anger only hurts you, not them. Remember that sometimes expecting abusive family members to apologise or make amends, will likely only give them the chance to blame you more if you attempt to hold them accountable.

We forgive others sometimes not because they deserve forgiveness, but because you deserve peace, and that wouldn't be achieved without forgiveness. We forgive because we are strong enough to know that people make mistakes, including us. I decided in my life to treat everyone with kindness and respect, even those who are rude to me, not because they are nice, but because I am. When you reach the blessing of forgiving someone, you can come to a point where you will not allow the other person to change who you are and that means that it doesn't matter what a person does, that means that you will not change your behaviour.

But remember that, forgiving people doesn't mean you agree with their behaviour; it is for you, so you can let it go and move on with your life.

The abuser's poor choices will not affect your personality, your choices. Whatever you do, don't wait to forgive someone until they apologise. If you wait for someone to acknowledge that they hurt you, you could be waiting forever and it puts them in the power position, where you need something from them in order to move forward in your life.

Forgiveness originates with self-love and is always an absolute for you. Boundaries are an essential part of forgiveness. Forgiveness doesn't excuse their behaviour. Forgiveness prevents their behaviour from destroying your heart.

Leaving and rebuilding life for the second time

Because I wanted so much to have quality time with him, I asked him if we would go on a cruise for our holiday. Joahnne could be having fun while we could finally have private time, kid free, for us to have intimate conversations and restore the long-time missing romance. Unfortunately by the time the cruising date arrived to embark, we were totally lost and unhappy; the situation between us was deteriorating quickly and again and I wasn't able to believe in his love anymore. I announced my intention to separate, we argued and one weekend I left home with Joahnne for a weekend at a friend's house. After many threats and discussions, Joahnne and I sailed without him to New Caledonia from 10 to 18 February 2013. Although for Joahnne it was an unforgettable time, for me what was supposed to be our happy family trip to celebrate and connect, was turned into a moment of deep grief and pain. He drove us to the pier but we embarked without money, carrying my father's credit card for basic needs. It was nice to have a week break cruising away from the cloudy environment at home, but also it was a turning point moment where I knew I was going to face another phase of crisis and difficult decisions and challenges when I returned. Sincerely in my heart, I was sorry. I remember I wrote a message to him on the sand, took a picture and sent it to him. When we were back to Sydney, he was there waiting to drive us home. I wanted to listen about his feelings and desires, but there was only silence. Despite the deep grief and suffering of the emotional situation again, about the need to make the decision to separate, at this time I was already aware, I knew where I was, what to do, where to go … I knew the road already. But, even not believing he would have an act of honour, I decided to fairly give him a chance of choice and called him for a conversation in front of the beach, before leaving. I asked him to leave the house this time, so Joahnne didn't need to leave her environment, her room, her routine.

Unfortunately the conversation didn't go well, his ego was dominating him and soon the conversation turned over to accusations and blaming, judging and put-downs. I was expecting a talk from the heart, but I received a talk from hate. So I just walked away from the hopeless conversation and made my decision to leave home again, accepting the offer of going to the women's refuge in Dee Why and start once more the journey of rebuilding the future.

The conversation was Friday and I left on Monday 25 February 2013, after a year of unsolved issues and seeing the abuse behaviour escalating. I was unfortunately called to take action and regain control of my life.

I left a letter for him trying to assure him to keep calm and remind him that this time the process was going to be not as traumatic as the first time. I said I was going to call him that night so he could say goodnight to Joahnne. I wasn't angry, I just wanted peace and since I wasn't seeing him collaborating to intimately connect, but letting his ego dominate his life, I felt forced to leave again to provide a healthier and happier environment for our daughter and myself. I was sorry because I so wanted my husband to be our warrior, our protector, our hero.

Joahnne and I went to Bringa, the Dee Why Women's Refuge. Within little more than one year of being reunited, it was well advised and predictable that the circle of the old pattern could easily return if not seriously respecting the 'rescue plan' we made at the end of 2011, designed by my social worker to safely start recovering our marriage through changing the way to approach conflict.

On refusing to keep attending couple counselling, church, our gospel reading together and especially the course at Relationships Australia about 'Taking Responsibility about violence', our plan of building a new relationship was failing. I was again feeling butterflies in my belly and my feminine instinct and all of my body senses were already sending me messages of fear – signs of crisis that was again arising. My emergency and alert system was turned on for protection; it was like watching the same movie again. So, before things escalated more, and to avoid more hurt, it was better to take action as the environment wasn't getting healthier, especially for what I believe my daughter deserves.

Too many things happened since then and Joahnne and I lived in the women's refuge for four months while I was rebuilding our life and looking for a home. To make things a bit more difficult for me, of course he denied my request to keep her in school by calling Joahnne's pre-school and cancelling the payment of the fees. Again I was quickly using all my connections to back her up and to be able to approve free childcare for her and avoid his poor decisions to affect her as little as possible.

Even with things like that, I was being civil and polite to him, trying to bring him to a bright side with peace. It was weird because publicly, it didn't appear that I was living with my daughter in a women's refuge, struggling financially, providing for her, covering needs, surviving a storm while everything in his life continued without change except that he was living alone in our unit. In less than a week, he rented Joahnne's room to someone. I thought that was really unfair for Joahnne and me. We were the ones living the heavy consequences because of his behaviour and irresponsibility. I was exhausted and had moments of heavy fatigue but was putting myself up and always okay for my daughter.

And yet, I was willing to meet him for lunch with Joahnne sometimes, I was being nice and easy with him when he was acting nice and trying to maintain for Joahnne the frame of Mum and Dad in her life being 'friendly' to each other and making her feeling loved by both. I was never asked if we needed anything, how we were living, or plans for future ...

the rare conversation, if any, was always shallow. I was failing to make him understand that we are family here and will be forever, that our original families are far away and that Joahnne has us two to count on and that we must to be able to count on each other, because if something happens to him I will be the one there for him and the reverse should be the same. Sometimes I was caught looking at him and feeling deeply sorry for our failure. The forgiveness was already in my heart and I was practising daily, sending love to him but knowing that the presence of his energy was very damaging and toxic, when he was living his inner crisis with rebellion.

In July of 2013, I finally could rent a unit after so many challenges of stress and hardship. While in the refuge I was again struggling, looking for solutions to rebuild life as quickly as possible and give Joahnne a new home. Here I was again, in a survival mode, dealing with financial approvals, Centrelink, countless meetings, options, healing counselling, spending hours awake searching for a home to provide for Joahnne. I had to give up my job to move to the Central Coast and began a whole new life with me studying at Tafe and Joahnne in a new school.

One day, Joahnne was sick and I called him to see if he wanted to visit but he said it was too far. Weeks later he called asking me for a sleep over, because he had a job to do in my area early in the morning and he could see Joahnne. I breathed deeply and said yes, against my emotional boundaries. Some months later, when he started to visit us more frequently, and we were spending time together with Joahnne, I had many moments being caught hoping that maybe he could still take real action to save his family who wanted to love him. Numerous times, we had good times with Joahnne having weekends as 'family' here in Gosford or in Dee Why at his house. Sometimes he used to withhold acting very strange, sometimes was acting nice and lovable and I was closely observing him. But the main point here is the sincere forgiveness that I hope one day he will find in his heart. During 2014 and up to Easter 2015, we had moments of intimacy and had signs of reconciliation. The trust was broken, but my heart was still playing with me. I felt he was playing happy family on the weekends he was meeting us, and then living his 'single life' during the week while I was dealing with all the responsibilities myself. I also planned a cruise together as a family, as the last hope of giving him a chance of speaking out his feelings and take action towards a solution of the actual situation we were living, and also to give us time to feel ourselves. It was still a battle to liberate myself from the marriage vows printed in my soul, from my truly intrinsic desires of seeing him acting with love toward me, fighting against the dream that all could be so different.

About Easter 2015, after really getting enough about many events, and allowing my heart to be continually toyed with, I made a decision to remove myself as a women from this unhealthy and hurtful relationship, but yet keep me there as a mother of our child and as a person/friend who deserves so much respect, trying to stop from that moment any physical approach when meeting each other to provide family environment and activities for Joahnne. Sometimes, when you finally give up on someone, it's not because you don't care anymore, but because you realise they don't.

Forgiveness has nothing whatsoever to do with how wrong you feel someone is treating you. No matter how evil, cruel, narcissistic or unrepentant they are. When you forgive a person you break the ties with the deeds that keep you in anguish. Forgiving breaks the unhealthy bonds between you and the abuser-victim relationship and redefines you as an independent victor in your own life.

Forgiving cuts the cord and leaves the abuser with the full weight of their deeds and fate and whether they accept their responsibility or not, you are no longer dependent on their participation in your healing. You can hold no malice, you can forgive them and you can then move on.

Anger is one of the most destructive, insidious feelings of all. Anger is responsible for broken relationships, sleepless nights, and high blood pressure. It destroys friendship, marriages and families, not to mention peace of mind. Anger is hard to handle for many people who have learnt from childhood that good people don't get angry. That's not true. Anger can show us that something is wrong and needs to be resolved and changed.

So why forgive? Forgiving is the only and unique thing that can free you from the anger that causes damage in every part of life. Forgiving will help you not let anger destroy your happiness and your health. Have compassion, because when someone is vicious to you they are giving you a glimpse of the pain that they carry in themselves. Viciousness is suffering. Be gentle when you can. If you are strong and safe in yourself then be patient and teach your virtues by your calm example.

How about trying to be less reactive and kinder to yourself and others. Start with learning to be light, having a smile of calm in your heart. Be peaceful. When you walk in peace, you will literally see attackers shattering themselves against your calm. They will defeat themselves. Some people cannot love us the way we want to be loved, because their heart is emotionally and spiritually frozen for whatever reason.

They require and then avoid affection. They will never be able to look deeply in your eyes, avoiding eye contact. They can be touching your hand with their hand but never with their heart. They will serve your body, but not your soul. They can only connect with you through futility, but never with passion, because they are empty inside. They are almost dead inside and they will break your heart if you let them. Be careful because you can waste your whole life waiting for them to wake up to the treasure that you have to offer to them.

Remember that inner peace begins the moment you choose not to allow another person or event to control your own emotions. While you are trying to turn crisis into blessings, forgiving is one of the biggest blessings you can find in your life, because when you are forgiving you're saving yourself, not the other person. When you are forgiving you are cleaning your soul from any kind of dark or negative feelings. If you'd like to make an exercise, make a list of all persons you have harmed and become willing to make amends to them all.

Offer forgiveness to those who have hurt you and make amends for harm you have done to others except when your soul would harm them or others.

When you are offering forgiveness and people are not able to receive your forgiveness, don't be angry with them, and just leave your gift there. Offer your forgiveness. What they are going to do is up to them. Through the process of forgiveness you will have to accept God's forgiveness. You will have forgiven others who have hurt you and you will have to forgive yourself, too. Because you may feel that the guilt and shame of your past is just too much to forgive, this is what God wants you to do with the darkness of your past. Isaiah 1:18 says, 'Come let's talk this over, says the Lord. No matter how deep the stain of your sins, I can take it out and make you as clean as freshly falling snow. Even if you're stained as red as crimson, I can make you white as gold, if you will only let me help you.' Through the process of forgiveness, you will achieve this state of grace and by grace you'll be saved through faith.

Forgiveness is one everlasting gift that you can offer to yourself and to others. Forgiveness provides an opportunity for us to exercise our capacity of forgiving. Think of it like this. To forgive can also mean to give before, and giving before basically means taking the initiative and being active. Forgiving can expand your capacity to love. Each time that we perceive forgiveness is required, that situation holds potentially wonderful growth and wisdom for us.

Whenever we feel forgiveness is needed, we are being given the opportunity to view the person as someone to be embraced in love. Forgiveness takes place through the energy of love. In everyday life we use the energy of love to clearly define and distinguish between others and ourselves and determine how close we allow others to us. When we learn to become more of our authentic selves and want balance, we expand our capacity to love.

The action of forgiveness in this manner is the balanced application of love. Remember that you can't change them, they can only change themselves, you can't force them, and they choose their own path. They can't create a loving relationship by themselves, you have to participate. You can't make them see their mistakes. Life does that for you later as it is not so much what happens on the outside that determines our destiny, it's our perception, decisions and actions that determine our outcomes.

We are not here to be victims of our story; we are here to be the big master of our destiny and forgiving is one important process of this path. One event or experience can be perceived as stressful or blissful depending on your perceptions and attitudes. The quality of your life is based on the quality of the questions you ask yourself.

If you ask questions that help you see how the experience will be valid, you are transforming stress into blessing. In the process of forgiveness, you'll be willing to look at another person's behaviour, as a view of the reflection of the state of their relationship with themselves, rather than as a statement as a value of your person. Then you will, over a period of time, cease to react at all. One of my social workers, one day she told me, the more chances you give someone, the less respect they will start to have for you. If you begin to ignore the standards you have set, then they know another chance will always be given.

They are not afraid to lose you, because they know no matter what, you won't walk away. They get comfortable depending on your forgiveness. Never let a person get comfortable with respecting you. Patience means being tolerant and forgiving. It means letting go of the anger and judgement, pain or discomfort, it is trusting that more will be revealed. Patience means looking for the lesson and blessing and knowing that you are being guided to a better life.

No woman can resist a loving, Godly man with a humble heart and sincere apology, taking responsibility for the damage they have done by their words and actions. I was touched by forgiveness when I felt that I was letting go of all the resentment, expectations and frustrations that were killing my soul and the real me.

When you hold negative feelings inside your mind and your heart and you do not allow yourself to forgive people or situations, actually you are hurting you and you'll be stuck in a situation where there is no growth and blessings. So get rid of all the anger, harsh words, bitterness, rage or any other evil feeling and exercise kindness to each other, try to soften your heart, forgiving each other just as you wish to be forgiven. And do it quickly for the sake of your own health.

Chapter 11

Touched by Gratitude

'Gratitude unlocks the fullness of life. It turns what we have into enough, and more. It turns denial into acceptance, chaos to order, confusion to clarity. It can turn a meal into a feast, a house into a home, a stranger into a friend.'

– Melody Beattie

Life will pay you whatever price you ask of it. The Bible says, 'Ask and you shall receive.' Ask intelligently and be grateful for anything you'll get back. Gratitude is an attitude that hooks us up to our source of supply and the more grateful you are, the closer you are to your maker, the architect of the universe, to the spiritual core of your being.

Be grateful and focus on your blessings, not on your misfortunes. Live your life with purpose. Focus on your strengths, not your weaknesses. Be yourself and don't wait for the approval of others, but most importantly have a positive and whole mindset no matter what situation you're in. Count your blessings, not your problems and you will realise how beautiful your life truly is and be grateful for that.

Be grateful for all relationships from your past and all the experiences and challenges you have faced before. The bad or the good. Everything you have experienced has lead to this moment. You have learnt or have grown and here you are still standing and still growing and be grateful for that.

In my experience of life, the more I was grateful the more I was receiving. The more I was thankful, the more I was receiving help to manage my problems. Years ago I learnt to have a gratitude journal where every day you write three things that you're grateful for. The gratitude journal can help you to recognise how many blessings you've been receiving from your life and when you start to read the journal with things that you've written before, you can see that you have many more blessings in your life than problems.

From when you wake up in the morning until the time you go to sleep, be grateful. Be thankful for God, be thankful for others, be thankful for your journey, be thankful for your food, your house and your life. Even if you're in a crisis situation and fighting or struggling to turn your crisis into blessings in your life, if you compare yourself with other people who are suffering much more in situations much more difficult, you will find the blessing and you will feel grateful for where you are.

Be thankful that you don't already have everything that you desire and if you did, what would there be to look forward to? Be thankful when you don't know something because it gives you the opportunity to learn. Be thankful for the difficult times, as in those times you grow. Be thankful for your limitations, because they give you opportunities for improvement.

Be thankful for each new challenge, because it will build your strength and character. Be thankful for your mistakes, they will teach you valuable lessons. Be thankful when you're tired and weary, because it means you have made a difference.

It is easy to be thankful for the good things; a life of rich fulfilment comes to those who are also thankful for their setbacks. Gratitude can turn a negative into a positive. Find a way to be thankful for your troubles, as they can become your blessings.

When you're asking something from the universe, remember to ask specifically: spiritual, relationship, financial, whatever. Remember to say why you are doing it. Give a big reason why you want it to happen. Ask what is your massive action plan to achieve what you're asking for? Through forgiveness and gratitude you will have a spiritual experience as a result of it. One of your jobs is to carry this message to others and practise these principles in all your affairs. Gratitude is a powerful process for shifting your energy and bringing more of what you want into your life. Be grateful for what you already have and you will attract more good things.

The affect of a grateful, thankful outlook on psychological and physical well-being was examined in several studies. In these studies participants were randomly assigned to groups and asked to keep daily records of their moods, coping behaviours, health behaviours, physical symptoms, and overall life evaluations. The gratitude-outlook groups exhibited heightened well-being across several, though not all, of the outcome measures across the studies, relative to the comparison groups. Results suggest that a conscious focus on gratitude and blessings will most likely have positive emotional and interpersonal benefits.

Gratitude or appreciation for the good things that happen in life is a really important part of building happiness. There are a number of benefits that can be gained from working gratitude into your everyday life. When you are exercising gratitude, you will appreciate the good things in your life, you will be boosting your mood, increasing positive feelings and coping better with tough times.

The benefits of gratitude can be a big list, but it's an instant mood booster and feels great in the moment. You are likely to feel closer to friends and family, you are likely to enjoy your life more, it's good for your physical health, it's easy to cope with tough times and good things in life don't stick in your head as easily as bad events.

There are three ways to increase your gratitude. As I said before, you can have a gratitude journal and take five minutes each day to have gratitude for what happened in your day. Take pictures; set yourself a mission to take photographs of things that are making you happy and tell someone how grateful you are about something that's happening in your life. Don't forget and remember that gratitude opens the doors to the power, the wisdom, the creativity of the universe, so you open the door to gratitude.

What are you grateful for today? Remember that it isn't happy people who are grateful but yet thankful people who are happy! I remember the power of gratitude in each situation I was facing in the past. I was always trying to be as grateful as possible for any favour or any person who was sending me something or giving me something that would help me to get through problems and make things feel lighter or easier. I was practising gratitude for each person I met, each organisation that was supporting me to be able to keep providing for my daughter.

And these days, I am also grateful for each blessed 'family moment' we can give to our daughter to honour and respect her like watching her gymnastics competitions or celebrating her special moments. I am grateful she receives her Child Support on time to support part of her needs, I am grateful I have the ability to no hold longer any harsh feelings against anyone and especially him, I am grateful when there is opportunity to relate in a helpful way making us accountable, I am grateful for any sign of respect and care. Thank you.

When we lower our expectations, we can find more gratitude. Being faithful and showing gratitude helped me to achieve all the basic needs that my daughter needed. In our worst moments, the basics were always provided as milk, nappies, food, furniture, childcare, money for activities. My God, I look back and can't believe how on earth I did it all! I couldn't believe that I was under a welfare system receiving from the shelter, the Salvation Army and St Vinnies in order to have enough to cover the basics of monthly living. And yet feeling so deeply blessed for it and for being able to be fully present in my daughter's daily life, building such a strong bond with her by providing all her emotional needs. I used any opportunity to show gratitude for any person who was giving me a hand.

To feel grateful is to feel thankful for something. Gratitude is a feeling of thankfulness. Gratitude is to express how pleasing someone's success is.

Luke 6:38 says, 'Give and it will be given to you. A good measure pressured down, shaking together and running over will be poured into your life for with the measure you see it will be measured to you.' Gratitude is a relationship strengthening emotion, because it requires us to see how we have been supported and affirmed by other people, because gratitude encourages us not only to appreciate gifts, but to repay them. Gratitude promotes forgiveness. Gratitude makes us pay it forward. Grateful people are more helpful, altruistic, or compassionate. Gratitude strengthens relationships. It makes us feel closer and more committed. Gratitude makes us more resilient. It has been found to help people recover from traumatic events. It has us thinking hard about our own mortality, makes us more grateful for life and other studies found that creating more will increase gratitude.

If you exercise and make a vow to practise gratitude, research shows that making an oath to perform increases the likelihood that the action will be executed. Therefore, write your own gratitude vow, which could be as simple as, *I vow to count my blessings each day*. And post it somewhere where you will be reminded of it every day.

Be thankful for what you have. You end up having more. If you concentrate on what you don't have, you will never have enough. When you come from an abusive relationship or an unhealthy relationship you can find it very hard to be grateful for it. But I assure you, if you keep growing and keep developing your personal and spiritual skills, you will for sure find gratitude in each thing that's happening in your life. You're going to be able to see clearly and see with your heart what could be behind that problem that you are facing.

When you can feel the gratefulness and thankfulness, you will start to count your blessings. Note the simple pleasure and acknowledge everything you're receiving. It means to live your life as if everything were a miracle and being aware on a continuous basis on how much you have been given. Gratitude shifts your focus from whatever your life lacks to the abundance that is already present.

One of the exercises that I learnt to do is to write a gratitude letter to a person who has exerted a positive influence in your life, but one who you have not properly thanked. Some gratitude experts suggest that you set up a gratitude meeting with this person and read the letter to them face to face. Once you appreciate what you have around you to be grateful for, you will find that you will not take special pleasures for granted. Gratitude should not be just a reaction of getting what you expect, but the ability to constantly look for the good, even in unpleasant situations. Today, start bringing gratitude to your experiences, instead of waiting for a positive experience in order to feel grateful.

There is always, always, always something to be thankful for. We've got to look for the good in the bad, the happy in the sad, the gain in your pain and what makes you grateful, not hateful. When you are grateful, fear disappears and abundance appears. Be grateful every morning when you wake up. For one day, each day in your life is a gift that you receive. Don't take it for granted.

During my journey I was always grateful for the people who make me happy, because they were the charming gardeners of my soul.

Chapter 12

Touched by Recovery

'Recovery is the healing process of your subconscious bringing wisdom to your conscious, helping you to restore your heart, reminding you to truly and honestly become the best version of you and achieving your full potential in life.'

– Luciane Sperling

Recovery is something that you have to work on every single day and it's something that doesn't get a day off. Remember that you can't solve problems by using the same thinking pattern you were using when the problem was created, or you will create yet more problems. Recovery is not going to be easy, because facing yourself requires big courage. But I'm telling you, it's going to be worth it. Remind yourself that hardships often prepare ordinary people for an extraordinary destiny. The recovery process will guide you to love yourself again, discover that you can trust yourself and take care of your happiness regardless the situation around you. You can find out that what you really need is to nurture your body and your spirit.

In August 2013, after moving to the Central Coast, where I found a new place to call home for me and my daughter, I bought a present for myself, which is a bracelet with the words '*This too shall pass*' and it reminds me that it doesn't matter what happens, good or not so good, life is a cycle and filled with phases, and each phase has a beginning and an end, opening the road to another beginning. I will remember that I must enjoy each experience and moment that is presented to my life and be grateful understanding that this too shall pass one day, and accept that! Things come and go, people come and go and you can only do the best that you are capable of based on the level of capability that you can, which will depend on your ability to the openness to learn.

Owning your story and loving yourself through the process is the bravest thing that you will ever do, because life will always offer you another chance.

I choose to dive into the process of recovery because I choose happiness and peace, and I had a goal to provide happiness and peace for my daughter. I choose positivity towards life, and I choose to look back into my core and honour who I am regardless the opinion of negative and judgmental people around me. From every wound there is a scar and every scar tells a story, a story that says: I have survived and I did my best. Turn your wounds into wisdom, because through wisdom you will understand that recovery is an ongoing work, it's a process, it's worth it and it's possible.

Believing in yourself and working on your recovery is the most important step in achieving the life you desire for yourself, for your kids and the life that you are worthy of and deserve. According to the dictionary, recovery is a restoration to a former or better condition. Remember that recovery is about progression, not perfection and often people who criticise your life are usually the same people *who don't know the price you paid to get where you are today.*

Perfection doesn't exist as we are just human beings, and if we were perfect, we would not be living in this world according to the divine justice. We are living in this world to learn about our mistakes, and we learn through connections and through relationships. Understanding what and why something is happening to us is the first step to acceptance, and only through acceptance the recovery can occur.

It hasn't been easy for me, but I was keen to look for answers choosing a number of options available throughout many organisations. The last three years I have been on a long journey of discovery while dealing with the deep grief of something that in my heart I didn't really want to leave behind (the attached hope of 'family'). But recovery is about looking toward the future and remembering 'why' we are doing it. Recovery helped me allow to turn myself into a new improved woman and to be in touch again with my values and my truth, living on purpose in the full life that I am supposed to live, because I believe that the law of attraction is impersonal and whatever we focus on we bring to us.

People would ask me: are you fully healed from the trauma, feeling of being betrayed, crisis and challenges you went through?

Well, one day I deeply believed and took seriously the vows of 'In the name of God, I, Jose, take you, Luciane, to be my wife, to have and to hold from this day forward, for better or worse, for richer or poorer, in sickness and in health, to love and to cherish all the days of my life. This is my solemn vow.'

The vow was holding my heart back for years. Family was always where I feel grounded and it is the essence of who I am. For me, family is the biggest treasure and responsibility we have in the world, to be protected no matter what and forever. Family is our primary place of learning and growth. I wanted to protect it with all my heart. So the answer to this question by today is honestly 'no', I am still in the process of healing because the scars remain, it is an ongoing process. And it is OK! I just found a way to live with the scar, forgiving and handling it with care and respect, while focusing my mind and heart on something much more rewarding towards the future: our daughter! She is the eternal symbol and seed of the vows made one day in heart and soul in the name of God, which will remain in our hearts. This is a very strong bonding that will never fade away. And because I am aware of that, and also because of my spiritual belief, we will always be part of this family forever, even if we put third parties in our future lives because the law of man does not separate what God has joined together in the hearts. Our wedding music lyrics can still make me cry, and it is okay because I respect that. It takes a long journey of recovering from wishing to hide the story or remove the person from myself to the level of owning and honouring it. Today I still have challenges to deal with, especially when there is lying and false or omitting events which disrespects what I am trying to build and can just bring us more problems in the future. But each of us makes our own choices and has consequences for them, although we are all just trying our best and the 'best' has different meaning to each one of us. But our daughter is the seed and strength of our eternal bridge who symbolize the real meaning of love as she is our miracle reminding us what is really worthy fighting for. The ongoing process of healing still continues and battles inside my core because the grief of having the dream family wiped out is a big deal for my family values, especially when I remind myself about the serious and hurtful reasons that made it happen. But, working in deep recovery, when we get to the point to understand the real meaning of forgiveness, we will be able to remove from our sight all the negative clouds of betrayal, anger, resentments, indignation, humiliation, pain of mistreatment, frustrations of not having the family succeeded as we believed it could, and many other suppressed feelings presented and covering the blue sky.

In reality, when we remove all those feelings and nasty events covering the precious essence and be really true to ourselves, we can clearly see each other with fraternal loving eyes, because the universal Godly love is still there, behind all of that bad stuff, printed somehow deeply in our soul forever, suffocated and put aside in the corner for not having permission to be alive and shine to be all that could have been. Because real love is something that has no end but we have power to decide what to do with it, live it or leave it. Acceptance about that requires big courage and profound honesty, and that means that moving forward from that will get easier in time.

Whenever you find yourself doubting how far you can go, just remember how far you have come. Remember everything you've faced, all the battles you have won and all the fears you have overcome. The recovery process will help you to stop hanging onto the past or fantasising, dreaming, wishing and replaying it again and again in your head. That was happening to me all the time. The worst feeling is the feeling of being attached to the good memories that are registered in your soul, the deep desire to live those emotions again, and instead being forced to not be able to live those feelings or express your love because of circumstances out of your control and healthier choices you must take for you or your kids.

Sometimes we just haven't realised it yet, but we already have moved on. You don't need what the past has; your life is here today. Your greatest moments are ahead of you and are right where you are now, so seize them while you can, before it's too late.

The process of recovery will help you to leave the old events behind to open space to create the new events. Trusting again to recreate yourself will help you let go of all the old life, like trauma, scars, memories, and old dreams holding you back. Ask yourself, 'What are the physical, emotional and mental steps to recover? What does your new life look like? Are you going to do it on your own? Which challenges will you face in the recovery process?' Have those questions in mind and if you can exercise answering them you will face your fears to walk the path of real recovery.

You will be trained to be stronger and that nothing can disturb your peace of mind anymore. Look at the sunny side of everything and make your optimism come true. Think only of the best, work only on the best, forget mistakes of the past and press on the greater achievements of the future. Give so much time to the improvement of yourself that you have no time to criticise others. Live in the faith that the whole world is on your side as long as you are true to the best that is in you.

As you continue to grow and heal, you attract those people who love you for who you are and you will tell yourself, *I no longer need to maintain abusive relationships.* I have no need to deny my feelings or to disguise my thoughts and beliefs. You will discover you are no longer tolerating people who put you down, manipulate you or who humiliate you. You surround yourself with people who are consistently loving and respectful. You will pursue people with whom you can share yourself totally with the complete assurance that they are accepting you for yourself alone.

You will have the courage to end relationships with people who are critical or not accepting of your real you, even loving them, because you will decide to love yourself more than them. The world is populated with self-respecting people who carry respect and return it back to you. Believe in that and you will attract them.

If you are depressed you are living in the past. If you are anxious you are living in the future. If you are at peace you are living in the present. In my recovery process I worked on myself to be the best version of me that I could be, to myself, to my daughter, to the world around me.

At beginning of January 2015, I got Joahnne to have fun and connect with kids who, as she does, receives the teachings of God. It was the Summerfest event at the EV Church on the Central Coast. They had workshops for parents as well and they were running the recovery program throughout the year. It is three terms, once a week in the morning, where you meet lovely people who are trying to recover themselves from different ranges of trauma. The 12-step program provides a path of recovery that's spiritually based, but not really religious. Working the steps of the program and practising the principles in all our affairs is a way of life that can relieve us from suffering, fill up the emptiness inside you and help you to discover yourself and the God within. The steps of recovery are designed to help keep people balanced. Members of the group will share their own experience.

Doing my research beyond the recovery program, I learnt that the recovery process is adapted for spiritual healing and also well used at Alcoholics Anonymous. The road of recovery has eight principles based on the beatitudes, created by Pastor Rick Warren and 12 steps with biblical comparisons.

So, learning that we are powerless over addictions including love addiction and admitting that our lives can become unmanageable, we have a choice to believe that there is a power greater than ourselves and this power could restore our sanity. I learned making decisions to turn my life and my will over to the care of God. I learned to make a fearless moral inventory of myself. I learned to admit to God, to myself and to other people the nature of my wounds. I learned that we are entirely ready to have God remove all these defects of character that we have. I learned to be humble in asking him to remove my shortcomings. I learned to make a list of persons that I had harmed and became willing to make amends to them.

I learned to make direct amends to such people whenever possible accept when to do so would injure them or others. I learned to continue to take personal inventory and when I was wrong, promptly admit it. I sought through prayer and meditation to improve my conscience of the universe, praying only for knowledge of his will, for us and power to carry that out.

And having had one more deep spiritual experience as a result of the steps, I tried to carry this message to others and to practise these principles in all of my affairs. For sure 2015 was a very important, remarkable year in my life. It was the year of construction, not just for doing the recovery program in the church, but also being open and courageous to face my fears of writing this book and sharing my experience with people around the world.

I can tell you it's not easy to be sitting at the position I am now. It is a very delicate situation to expose a bit of my path without hurting someone but my main goal is to be one more drop in the ocean, stepping up for the justice and the awareness of women and children being hurt around the world, and families being destroyed each day due to a lack of a system to heal the root of the cause. I haven't been sleeping much the last months going through an emotional journey on the calling received to put this book out to the world to share the experience of growth through the process of my healing. Everything this year was being revealed to me week by week to culminate to today's day. I believe I have been called to this moment, as I am receiving messages through my dreams and people around me.

Those messages I am receiving look like a truly burning desire that wakes me up in the middle of the night to write and make notes. I feel that I've learnt and I grew so much and the more we grow and learn, the more we realise that we have so much still to grow. We realise how small we are, but as someone said to me one day, the ocean is big, but be a drop in the ocean and that drop will resonate in the rest of the ocean and will affect others touching and making a difference in their lives.

Many times I found myself avoiding this book for weeks because of the fear of digging emotions or sharing my thoughts and feelings and I was wondering how I would share a little bit of my story without confronting anyone that was related to the story of my life. My intention here is not to hurt anyone, but yes to heal myself and yes to support and help other women who could be facing similar situations to what I have faced, so my expectation is to remind you that recovery is the process of growth.

Finally, I was touched by recovery, because through the recovery process I could understand the situation and myself much better and have more compassion and patience for who gets lost on those clouds being unable to see and live the essence. Through recovery, I am glad that we are able to have and give a 'good' time together with Joahnne and glad when he is willing to use his heart in those moments. I don't like to follow protocols when it comes to our children, but what comes from the heart and from good intention for their best happiness, not forcing them to do what their heart is not asking for. My road is based in love and peace and I will not drive off that path.

At any given moment, you have the power to say, 'This is not how my story is going to end.' I am investing in myself to be able to serve people around me and live my life with purpose, and be a valuable figure to the community.

To end this chapter, I would like to leave here some life changing principles to hold in your heart:

- ✓ Be grateful and say 'hello' and 'thank you' often with kindness.
- ✓ Learn to forgive people, and yourself.
- ✓ Be always honest and frank when expressing your self – with kindness.
- ✓ Practise random acts of kindness, especially for the ones who you have an energy conflict.
- ✓ Be generous.
- ✓ Focus on what you are good at.
- ✓ Give the world the best you have.
- ✓ Create a healthy social network for yourself.
- ✓ Show love, it's a doing word.
- ✓ You can have it all, just not all at once.

LIGHT YOUR LIFE

Afterword

'Within you is the divine capacity to manifest and attract all that you need or desire.'

– Wayne Dyer

The greatest loss in life is not death. Loss is when life dies inside you while you are alive, so remember to keep your heart soft and alive making sure that the past has no power and no hold over you anymore. We can live the half-experienced life or we can live the full and blessed life we were given. Learning how to impress the creator instead of His creatures may be the vision we need to deal with the challenges presented to our lives. The choice of the emotional state you choose to mentally connect with, will be the turning point between the good or the bad choices in your day-by-day living. Altering perceptions and attitudes of mind is the only way to achieve your full potential as a human being, working to stop being a slave to your own negative mindset living in an illusory prison. Negative talk and negative mindset will only keep you from receiving all the love and all the blessings you could be receiving.

I hope that, on finishing reading this humble book, you may at some point realise that it's not so much what happens on the outside that determines our destiny, but yes our perceptions, decisions, and actions that determines our outcomes. You are here not to be victims of your history, but the hero survivor and the master of your destiny. Any experience can be both perceived as stressful or a blessing and as a hole or a bridge, depending on your perceptions and attitude. Once the storm is over you perhaps won't remember how you made it through or how you managed to survive. You perhaps won't even be sure, in fact, if the storm is really over. But be sure that once you come out of the storm, you won't be the same person who walked in. Writing this book was one of the steps of my emotional recovery towards a better me.

Take chances and be brave to take a lot of them without procrastinating. Because honestly, no matter where you end up and with whom, it will end up just the way it should be. Our mistakes and successes make us who we are. If you are wise, you will learn and grow with each choice you make. Everything is worth it. Say how you feel, always. Be you, and be okay with it.

Please remember the quality of questions you ask yourself, so that by asking yourself the right questions it will help you to see the outer negative experiences, which will serve to your highest values, and you will be able to transform crisis into blessings with kindness.

Love & Light,

Luciane

Touching your Senses

'I don't know what your destiny will be, but one thing I know: the only ones among you who will be really happy are those who will have sought and found how to serve.'

– Albert Schweitzer

Sometimes when we are struggling through bad times, it is important to look for comfort, inspirations and encouragement. Here I would like to share some of the positive ways I found very useful to boost my senses and help me to surround my life with goodness.

Searching for the best tools to fill your life with greatness can make a big difference when it comes to create your emotional mindset. Real-life survival stories, books, music, and films can really help you to find strength and motivation, finding yourself thinking outside your own box and often remind you that you are not alone in your suffering.

Books

I love to read three categories of books: the real-life stories (which can bring deep life experiences, showing how much courage people are capable of), books of affirmations (which can give a reminder to stay strong and grounded) and self-help books (which gives the tools and skills to cope with unfamiliar situations).

- *The Holy Bible*
- *Stronger than you think*, by Kim Gaines Eckert
- *The Verbally Abusive Relationship*, by Patricia Evans
- *Inside the Mind of an Angry Man*, by Evan L. Katz, M.C., LPC
- *How to bounce when others break*, by Dr. Steve W Price
- *The Magic of the Moment*, by Maggie Hamilton
- *The Millionaire Messenger*, by Brendon Burchard
- *The Mum Factor*, by Dr Henry Cloud and Dr John Townsend
- *Boundaries with Kids*, by Dr Henry Cloud and Dr John Townsend
- *The Book of Forgiving*, by Desmond Tutu and Mpho Tutu
- *The Gospel According to Spiritism*, by Allan Kardec

- *Set Yourself Free*, by Shirley Smith PhD with Shelley Neller
- *The Secret*, by Rhonda Byrne
- *The Motivation Manifesto*, by Brendon Burchard
- *What Motivates Me*, by Adrian Gostick and Chester Elton
- *The Five Love Languages*, by Gary Chapman
- *The Seven Principles for Making Marriage Work*, by John M Gottman PhD
- *The Dip – A Little book that teaches you when to quit (and when to stick)*, by Seth Godin

Music

Music can be very inspiring and is like food for the soul, because has the power of arouse different feelings through the meaning or significance in song lyrics.

- *Beautiful* by Christina Aguilera
- *Misty Eyed Adventures* by Maire Brennan
- *Survivor* by Destiny's Child
- *Hero* by Mariah Carey
- *Rise and Fall* by Craig David featuring Sting
- *Believer* by Christine Milian
- *Roar* by Katie Perry
- *Where do I go from Here* by Judy Kuhn, Pocahontas
- *For Once in My Life* by Stevie Wonder

Films

I love powerful films, which you can learn and think about afterwards. I also like to watch some of the modern kids' films with my daughter, which we can relate to real life.

- *Forrest Gump*, starring Tom Hanks
- *Erin Brockovich*, starring Julia Roberts
- *Home Run*, directed by David Boyd
- *A Beautiful Mind*, starring Russel Crowe
- *Philadelphia*, starring Tom Hanks
- *The Blind Side*, starring Sandra Bullock
- *Dangerous Minds*, starring Michelle Pfeiffer
- *Dead Poets Society*, starring Robin Williams
- *The Shift*, starring Wayne Dyer

Positive learnings

When we focus on excellence on the positiveness through role models, we surround ourselves wisely with good gems. There are a number of websites focusing on self-esteem and happiness, spirituality, abundance, self-development and countless information of wellness. Also the value you will get with the knowledge and vision of amazing national and international leaders who makes a difference to millions of people's lives is priceless.

Here are some of the ones I am personally following and I hope you enjoy:

- www.joycemeyer.org
- www.drwaynedyer.com
- www.drdemartini.com

- www.tonyrobbins.com
- www.petakelly.com
- www.virgin.com/richard-branson
- www.johnassaraf.comwww.actionforhappiness.org
- www.projecthappiness.com
- www.ted.com

Resources and Support

Getting Connected

What can you do now, if you feel you or someone you know needs support? Please, look in your area and community for the supporting organisations related to your need. You will be amazed to get to know how much support there are out there.

Refuges and shelters

Many organisations provide safe and secure refuges, shelters, or emergency accommodation for women and children escaping domestic violence. They assist women with emotional support, legal assistance, help with finding permanent housing and applying for appropriate benefits. The location of some refuges is kept secret to protect the safety and security of women and children residents. For this reason, referral to refuges and shelter will be needed.

My local Support was:

Salvation Army (www.salvationarmy.org.au) and St. Vincent de Paul (www.vinnies.org.au) can assist you in many issues like legal advice, food vouchers, EAPA vouchers, referral letters, accommodation, employment, financial assistant and other issues. Please go to the website and find out more and your nearest centre.

The Central Coast Community Women's Health Centre provides short-term counselling and support by trained counsellors who draw upon a variety of counselling and therapeutic approaches that have proven to be useful in assisting women to better understand their experiences and help move them towards resolution and healing.

White Ribbon (www.whiteribbon.org) is a primary prevention campaign working to change the attitudes and behaviours that lead to violence against women, and as consequence of many social problems. If you or someone you know is experiencing violence and need help or support, please contact one of the support services below. There are national and state-based agencies that can assist you 24 hours a day, 7 days a week.

National Hotlines – Counselling and Support

1800 RESPECT (1800 737 732): 24 hour, National Sexual Assault, Family & Domestic Violence Counselling Line for any Australian who has experienced, or is at risk of, family and domestic violence and/or sexual assault. www.1800respect.org.au

Lifeline has a national number who can help put you in contact with a crisis service in your State
13 11 14 (24 hours) www.lifeline.org.au

Police or Ambulance
000 in an emergency for police or ambulance.

Translating and Interpreting Service
Phone 131 450 to gain access to an interpreter in your own language (free)

Suicide Call Back Service 1300 659 467

Mensline Australia
Supports men and boys who are dealing with family and relationship difficulties
Ph: 1300 78 99 78 (24/7) www.mensline.org.au

Kids Help Line
Telephone counselling for children and young people
Freecall:1800 55 1800
E-mail and web counselling www.kidshelp.com.au

Australian Childhood Foundation
Counselling for children and young people affected by abuse
Freecall: 1800 176 453 or (03) 9874 392. Email:info@childhood.org.au. www.childhood.org.au

Relationships Australia
Support groups and counselling on relationships, and for abusive and abused partners.
Ph:1300 364 277. www.relationships.com.au

Blue Knot Foundation (formerly Adults Surviving Child Abuse)
Telephone counselling for adult survivors of childhood trauma, their friends, family and the health care professionals who support them.
Blue Knot Helpline: 1300 657 380 (9am-5pm 7 days)
Email:helpline@blueknot.org.au Website: www.blueknot.org.au

National Disability Abuse and Neglect Hotline
An Australia-wide telephone hotline for reporting abuse and neglect of people with disability.
1800 880 052. www.disabilityhotline.org

Safe Relationships Project
Provide men and women who are experiencing domestic violence in Same Sex relationships with support, advocacy, referral and information.

Referral and information about seeking referral:

Australian Government Department of Health Services
Family and domestic violence
www.humanservices.gov.au

Healthdirect Australia
Healthdirect Australia is a non-commercial, government funded organisation providing trusted health information to all Australians.
http://www.mindhealthconnect.org.au/abusive-relationships

LGBTIQ Domestic Violence Information:

National Police Assistance line: 131 444. Some Police stations have an LGBTI liaison Officer (known as GLLO/Gay and Lesbian Liaison Officer).

Another Closet Online resource with information and referral details on LGBTIQ domestic and family violence. www.anothercloset.com.au

State and Territory Helplines

If you want help or information for yourself or someone else, here are the contact details for the domestic violence help lines for each State and Territory. You can contact them 24 hours a day.

Australian Capital Territory

Domestic Violence Crisis Service (DVCS)
02 6280 0900. www.dvcs.org.au

Canberra Rape Crisis Centre (CRCC)
Crisis support, counselling, advocacy and support programmes for women and men. 02 6247 2525 (7am-11pm). Text Only 0488 586 518. www.crcc.org.au

Everyman Australia (formerly Canberra Men's Centre)
02 6230 6999. www.everyman.org.au

New South Wales

NSW Domestic Violence Line
Provides telephone counselling, information and referrals for women and same-sex partners who are experiencing or have experienced domestic violence. 1800 65 64 63. 1800 671 442 TTY (Hearing impaired). 24/7.

Rape Crisis Service
1800 424 017 (24/7 Counselling)

Interrelate Family Centres
1300 736 966. (02) 8882 7800. www.interrelate.org.au

Link2home: A statewide homelessness information and referral telephone service. 1800 152 152 (24/7). http://yfoundations.org.au/need-help/yconnect/

Northern Territory

Domestic Violence Crisis Line
1800 019 116

Sexual Assault Referral Centre
08 8922 6472

Queensland

Domestic Violence Telephone Service
1800 811 811

Sexual Assault Help Line
1800 010 120

Men's Info Line
1800 600 636

QLD DV WebLink (a directory of QLD support services)
www.qlddomesticviolencelink.org.au/

South Australia

Domestic Violence Helpline
1300 782 200

Yarrow Place Sexual Assault Service
1800 817 421

Tasmania

Family Violence Counselling and Support Service
1800 608 122

Family Violence Response & Referral
1800 633 937

Sexual Assault Support Service
03 6231 1817

Men's Line Australia
1300 364 277

Victoria

Safe Steps Family Violence Response Centre
1800 015 188 or 9322 3555

Sexual Assault Crisis Line
1800 806 292

Men's Referral Service
1800 065 973

Western Australia

Women's Domestic Violence Helpline
08 9223 1188/ 1800007 339

Crisis Care
1800 199 00808 or 9233 1111

Sexual Assault Res. Centre
08 9340 1828 or 1800 199 888

Men's Helpline
08 9223 1199 or 1800 000 599

Legal Advice (visit websites for more information)

Legal Aid NSW
Call 1300 888 529

Legal Aid ACT
Call 1300 654 314

Legal Services Commission of South Australia
Call 1300 366 424

Victoria Legal Aid
Call 1300 792 387

Legal Aid WA
Call 1300 650 579

Legal Aid QLD
Call 1300 651 188

Northern Territory Legal Aid Commission
Call 1800 019 343

Legal Aid Commission of Tasmania
1300 366 611

Additional Services

To find contact details and links to more organisations refer to the **Domestic Violence Resource Centre** www.dvrcv.org.au

NSW Victims Services Mobile app, The Justice Journey, has been designed to reduce the stress often experienced by victims involved in the criminal justice system, and provides information and guidance for victims from the time they become a victim until after the court process has finished. www.victimsservices.justice.nsw.gov.au/Pages/vss/vs_justicejourney/VS_justicejourney.aspx

Daisy is an app that connects women around Australia to services. www.1800respect.org.au/daisy

The Immigrant Women's Health Service (IWHS) was established in 1987 to address the needs of immigrant and refugee women in regard to health information and health services. Visit: http://www.immigrantwomenshealth.org.au/

Our Watch has been established to drive nation-wide change in the culture, behaviours and attitudes that lead to violence against women and children. www.ourwatch.org.au

Sponsors and Non-profit Partners

I will be forever grateful for your generous sponsorship, donations and network support, which granted the real feeling of this book becoming a reality. Thank you for your care forever.

My special gratitude goes to Melissa Polwarth, Jon Chin, Hamish Bruce, Bruce Dent and Matt Hodgson.

The Hunter TAFE Foundation is a not-for-profit, charitable organisation working with Hunter business, education and community leaders committed to supporting education and training at Hunter TAFE by helping students achieve their goals.

The Hunter TAFE Foundation was established in 2000 to accept donations from business and community to establish Awards, Scholarships and Grants to provide financial assistance and support to students studying at Hunter TAFE.

Since inception the Hunter TAFE Foundation has presented approximately $1.4 million in Awards, Scholarships and Grants to students who are either experiencing personal or financial hardship, or to acknowledge academic achievement.

The Hunter TAFE Foundation is committed to providing support and encouragement to students today, tomorrow and in the future

To find out more about the Hunter TAFE Foundation or to donate visit:

WWW.HUNTER.TAFENSW.EDU.AU/ABOUT-US/PAGES/FOUNDATION.ASPX

To donate to White Ribbon, please go to www.whiteribbon.org.au

International Day for the Elimination of
Violence Against Women
25 November

Hunter White Ribbon Day Committee

Aphrodite's Secret

In Greek mythology, Aphrodite is the Goddess of love.

Aphrodite's unbridled passion means lofty ideals such as liberation and renewal, energy and empowerment, ecstasy and oneness, both with others and with the divine.

You can become the woman you want to be.

www.aphroditessecrets.com.au

Essential Oil Based Perfume

To donate to St Vincent de Paul, please go to www.vinnies.org.au/donate or call 13 18 12

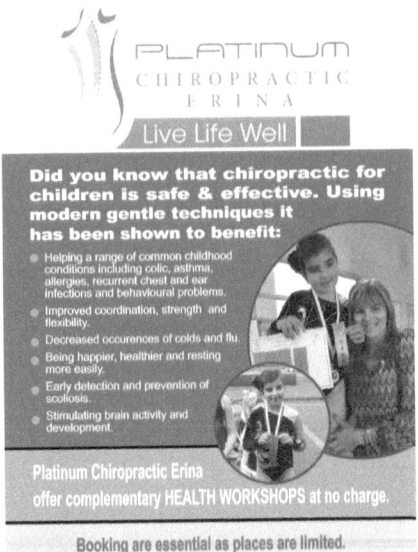

Appeal to Donate

Luciane aims to support local community through this book.

Coast Shelter is a not-for-profit charity based on the NSW Central Coast, which provides accommodation and support programs for people who are homeless or at risk of homelessness.

www.coastshelter.org

Ph: (02) 4325 3540

If you would like to make a difference to someone else life, please donate to Coast Shelter here: www.coastshelter.org.au/donation.html

Appendices

Safety Checklist
See safety strategies list

I will use the following prevention strategies:

To manage an emergency at home I will:

To manage an emergency in public I will:

To help my children to manage an emergency I will:

Safety Strategies

Tick those that are suitable for you.

'Technology' strategies

- ❏ Carry your mobile phone, <u>charged, and switched on, at all times</u>. Be confident about how to call emergency services from your handset.

- ❏ Program your mobile with all your emergency numbers (police, trusted friends and family members). Memorize emergency phone numbers in case you need to use a payphone or neighbours phone.

- ❏ If _____ starts abusive text messages, save text messages. Police can use these as evidence.

- ❏ Make sure that the passwords to your phone, email and bank accounts remain secret. Make sure that they are things that cannot be worked out. If you are emailing friends and family log of if you are leaving the computer unattended. This is a good habit to get into.

Financial Safety planning

- ❏ Cancel any shared credit cards, and open a new account at a different bank and keep the card at a friend's home and have bank statements delivered to a friend's home.

- ❏ If you are working, make sure your work in aware of your situation. Make sure that your wages go into your own bank account.

- ❏ Have a look at the information provided on relationship debt provided from office of fair trading and legal aid. Keep this information at a friend's house where you will continue to have access if required.

Safety planning to protect yourself inside the home

- ❏ Identify things that have worked in the past to keep you safe.

- ❏ Think about what has happened in the past and how the abuser has acted. Identify clues that indicate when things are about to get violent (i.e. holidays, body language, drinking). Remember that perpetrators of violence are not always predictable and that it is not always possible to predict when an event is going to occur.

- ❏ If a violent incident occurs or you are worried that it might, leave if you can. DO not wait until things have gotten out of control before you leave.

- ❏ If you are ever concerned that an incident may occur, keep away from rooms with weapons (such as the kitchen) and rooms with no exits (such as the bathroom)

- ❏ Know the easiest escape routes within the home – doors, windows etc. and teach your children these routes

- ❏ Think about where you would go if you needed to escape and who you would call. Make a plan and practice it.

- ❏ Ask your neighbours to call the police if they are worried about your safety. Make sure you know your new neighbours. Keep in mind that where you were previously you knew all your neighbours and a number of them were aware of the situation. It would be good to get to know your new neighbours to reduce the risk of losing the old neighbours who were a protective factor.

- ❏ Pack a bag with important things that you would need if you had to leave your home quickly, leave it in a safe place or with a friend or relative you trust. Include cash, a spare set of keys, some clothing for you and your children, as well as important documents including; court papers, copy of your ADVO, passports, birth certificates medical records (inc. children's 'blue books') medical records and medicines.

'Support' strategies

- ❏ Inform your neighbours that there is a history of violence. Ask them to call the police if they hear a disturbance at your home.

- ❏ Attend a support group with women who have had similar experiences. Keep in contact with your support services such as Angela.

- ❏ Arrange a password with your family or friends. In the event of an emergency, where it is not safe for you to call the police directly, you may be able to call a friend without attracting attention. Use the password to let them know that you are unsafe and that they should call the police.

- ❏ Keep your DV related information, particularly information with details of support services including ours at a friend's home.

- ❏ Keep a copy of your old AVO at the house in a place that you can get it if you need to provide it to the police. Keep in mind that it is common for perpetrators of violence to encourage women to throw away old documents or remove these documents without the woman's knowledge.

'Legal' strategies

- ❏ Always call the police if there is a breach of your ADVO or if you don't have one to arrange assistance if there has been violence. Make sure that they are aware of the history.

- ❏ Keep a diary of any abuse. Record anything that made you feel uncomfortable or unsafe. Write down the substance of any conversation, and any threatening or intimidating statements. This will be very helpful if you have to go to court.

- ❏ Keep a copy of your AVO with you e.g. in your handbag, at home, at work and with a trusted friend

Online Safety Strategies

- ☐ If you have been sharing a computer with the offender, be aware that both sent and received emails can be accessed along with a history of websites that you have visited. Empty your deleted items folder and your CACHE (the place where your computer stores all the information you have browsed) regularly so these cannot be accessed

- ☐ If you feel at all unsure that your computer is not a 'safe zone', then wherever possible use a friends computer, an internet café or the internet facility at your local library (often, a staff member at a library would be able to teach you how to empty your deleted items and your CACHE if your unsure)

Shark Cage

Below, find the concept for the Shark Cage, which I discussed in Chapter 8.

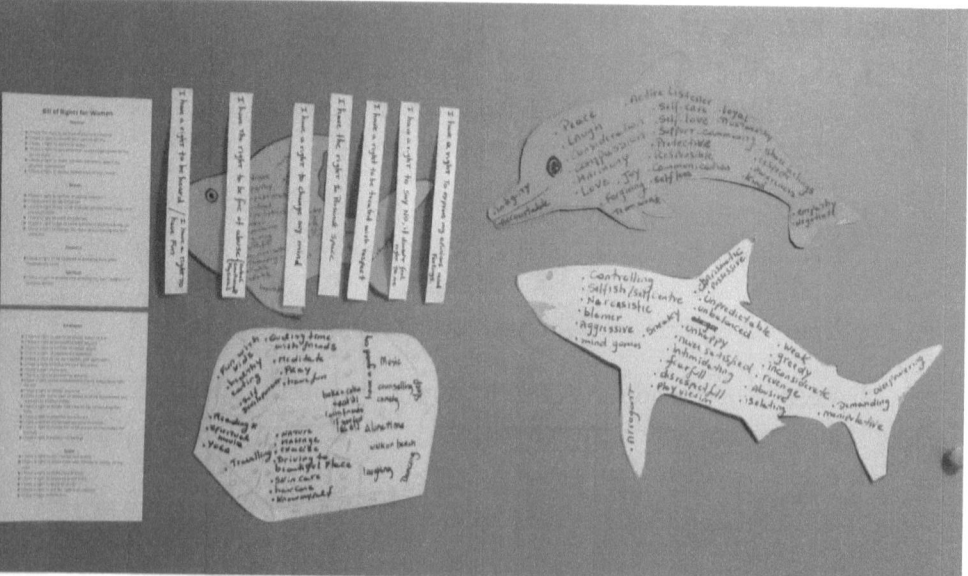

Exercises

These exercises will help you reach your past subconscious memories..

Life Evaluation Worksheet - The Events/People that have Hurt me

Column 1	Column 2	Column 3	Column 4
I feel bad about:	The Cause:	The Effect/Damage:	My Part:
(the specific pain, anger, hurt)	(the circumstances)	(the effect that had on my life) (to my basic social, security or sexual instincts)	(What part did I play in this if any?)

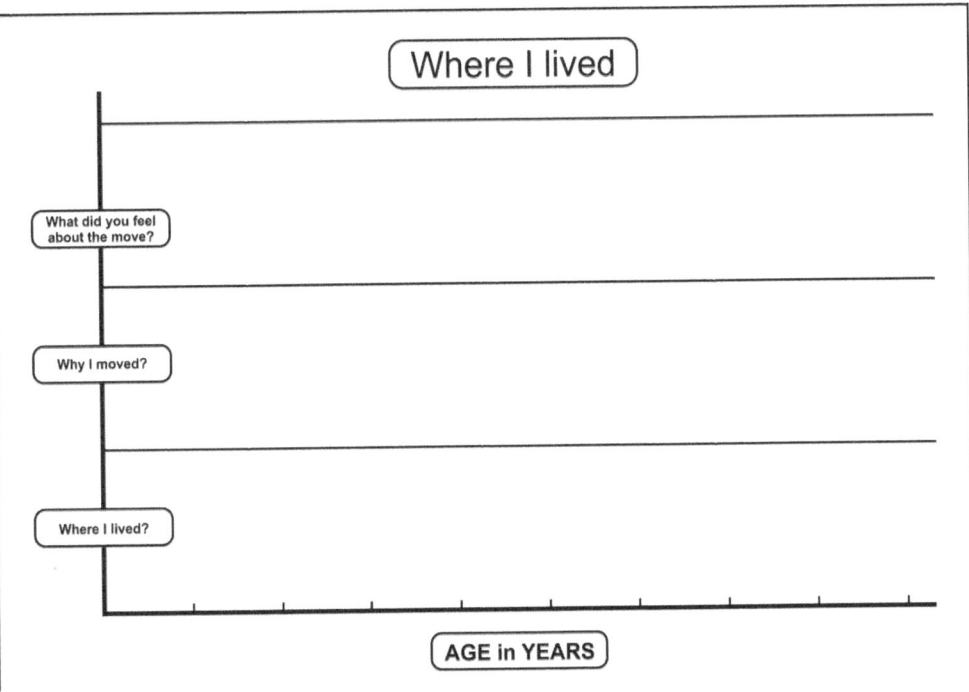

Diagrams

On the following pages, you'll find diagrams that explain concepts we've discussed throughout the book.

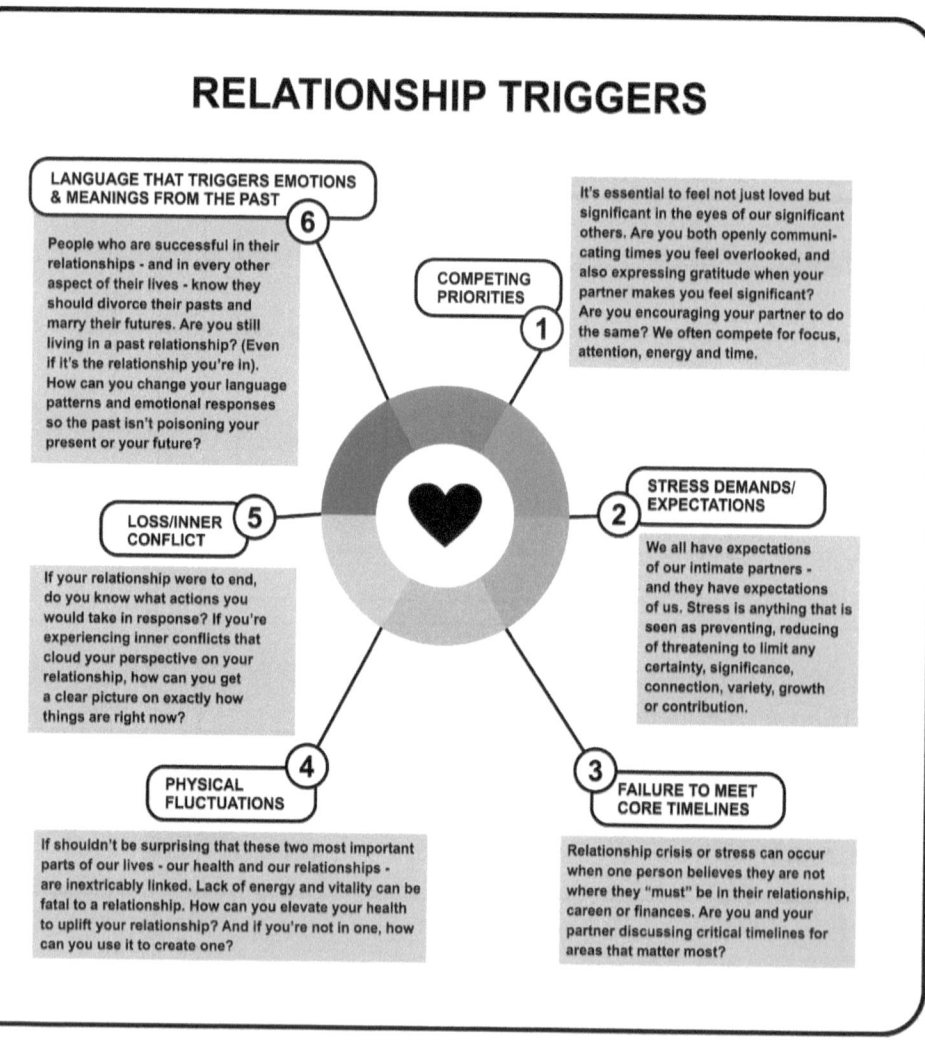

LIVING OUT THE FIVE LOVE LANGUAGES AT HOME

Love Language	Actions	Communication	Avoid
Words of Affirmation	Spoken words Written cards and letters	Encouraging words Compliments Affirming spirit	Emotionally harsh words Undue criticism
Quality Time	Running errands Talking trips Doing things together Going on walks Sitting/talking at home	Quiet places with no interruptions Undivided attention One-to-one conversations	Too much time with friends or groups Isolation Gaps of time between meetings
Receiving Gifts	Giving gifts Giving time Remembering special occasions Giving small tokens	Private giving of gifts Pleasant facial expressions	Materialism Forgetting special events
Acts of Service	Assisting with house chores Ongoing acts of helpfulness Exchanging of chores	Say: "What can I do for you?" "I will stop and get..." "Today, I did... for you." Making a checklist	Forgetting promises Over commitment of tasks Ignoring
Physical Touch	Hugs Pats Touches Sitting close	Pleasant facial expressions Mostly non-verbal	Physical abuse Corporal punishment Threat Neglect

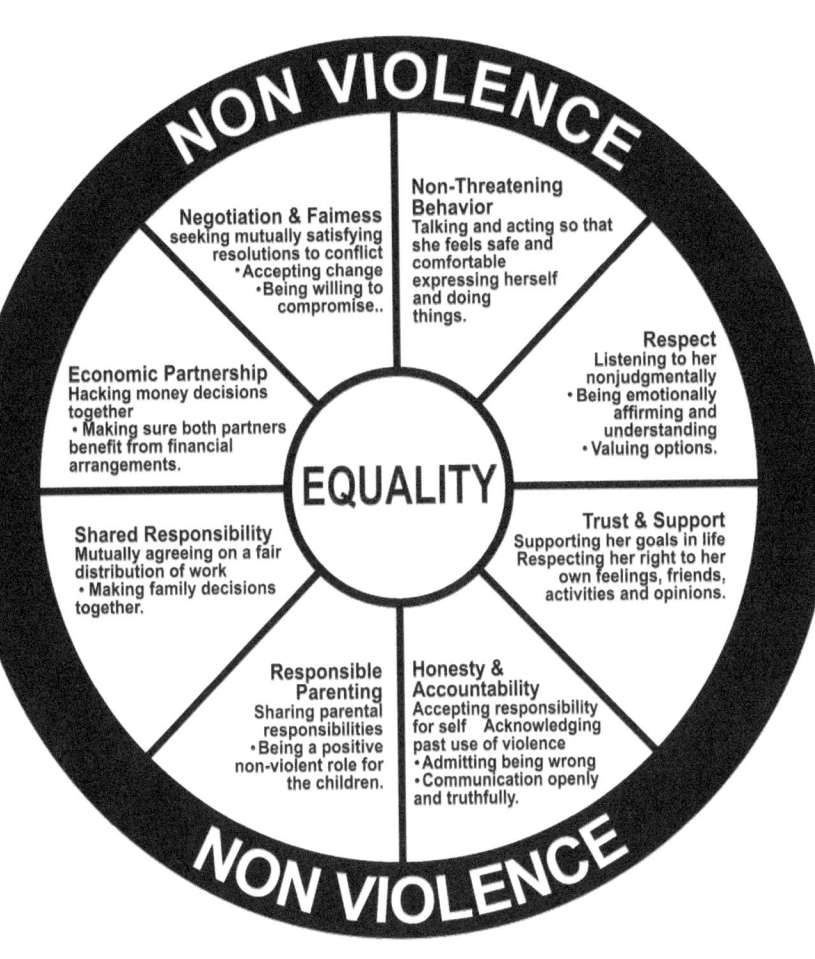

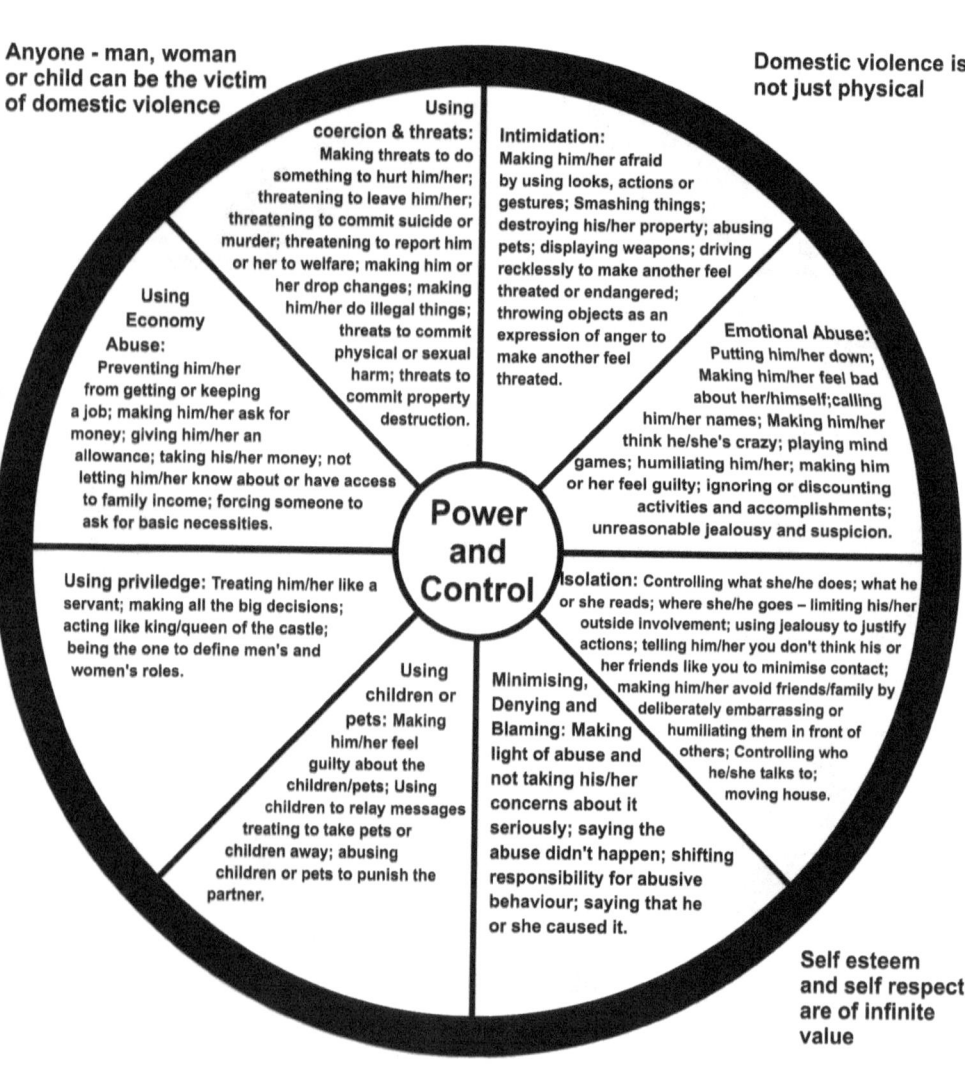

The cycle of Violence

Tension

This feels like walking on eggshells. Nothing is right. There is no way to predict what the abuser wants. While there may not be physical violence (or at least physical violence is minimal), there is emotional abuse, intimidation and threats. Fear of violence is often as coercive as violence itself.

As the cycle is repeated, the violence usually increases in frequency and severity.

Violence

This is the actual violent episode. It inlcudes physical, emotional or sexual abuse. A crime is committed.

The "Honeymoon"

Abusers act differently after violent episodes. Some ignore or deny the violence. Some blame their "anger" on something you said or did. Some fear losing you and act genuinely sorry. This phase is often called the "honeymoon". The abuser will try to make up for his violence. He may act sorry, send cards and flowers, buy presents, help around the house, spend time with his kids, go to church, get counselling, or make promises. The abuser may seek pity. It's important to realize that this phase is an attempt to draw you back into the relationship. This phase is never a real "honeymoon".

The more time the cycle is completed the less time it takes to complete.

About the Author

Luciane was born in Brazil and at the age of 37 she felt called to a new challenge with a big goal of living in a more developed country to study English, learn new skills and live in a safer environment with access to a higher quality of life. After closing her conference business, selling her home, her car and giving away her belongings, she migrated by herself to Australia in 2006.

With her heart believing she found the man who would care and love her forever, she married in 2008 and her sweetheart daughter was born in 2009. Since then Luciane has faced the biggest crisis of her life but also more blessings and opportunities that she possibly could count.

She has twice lived in a women's refuge after sadly being forced to leave her own home to protect herself and her daughter from an abusive environment. In the women's refuge she was stirred being surrounded by amazing women and their stories, which revealed to her a hidden world filled with women threatened and abused by their partners, yet trying their best to protect and provide for their children.

Luciane is a survivor of domestic violence who believes God gave her a mission to raise awareness using her experience to show women the road of recovery not only to survive, but to thrive, and that it is possible to turn any crisis into a blessing finding your inner peace even if the world is falling around you.

Since 2013, Luciane has lived on the beautiful Central Coast of NSW Australia where she is providing a happy and healthy life for her herself and her daughter.

Luciane founded *My Inner Light* with the purpose of bringing awareness about Domestic Violence and how you can recover and achieve your full potential as a human being.

Luciane Sperling is a heart centred faithful woman, loving and dedicated mother, a dreamer and doer with a strong sense of empathy, stern yet compassionate, believing that all things are possible.

Soon, her book *Touched by Love: Turning Crisis into a Blessing* will be translated into Portuguese and launched in Brazil.

About My Inner Light

Luciane Sperling is a founder of *My inner Light – awakening your inner self*. My Inner Light was created as a platform for education about unhealthy relationships, to empower and educate women to find their voice aligned to their truth and values, especially when experiencing abuse leading to domestic violence. *Touched by Love* is the first seed and product of this platform, with the objective to create educational programs for women and children.

Luciane has no intention to teach others but she is willing to turn her experience and knowledge gained through the years into something good to serve people, guiding or mentoring when they need it, if they are walking a similar experience in life. Luciane's aim is focused on family and community.

The Lotus Flower representing 'My Inner Light' logo is associated with purity and beauty, and has a very significant meaning because who ever observed a lotus flower emerging from a murky pond, will see the beauty of this plant always looking so clean and pure against the background of the dirty pond.

The different colours of the lotus flower represent different stages of spirituality:

Blue: symbolizes someone who has started their spiritual journey by leaving the concept of 'self' behind. It is symbolic with a victory over the spirit of self.

Pink: is the one reserved for enlightenment of the highest order and is associated with the highest divinity.

White: it is in a stage between blue and pink and is associated with the state of becoming awakened to the wonders of it all. When one reaches this state it is said that one has mental purity and has reached a state of spiritual perfection.

Connecting with Luciane

Luciane is trying to live as aligned as possible to a spiritual and healthy lifestyle bringing to her sweetheart Joahnne the best quality life she can possibly provide, showing that we can walk through life finding joy, serving the community, connecting with like-minded people and find magic in the most unexpected places and situations. She believes we are on this earth with the rare opportunity of connecting and learning with each other, and the result of those connections is to transform us into a better soul. For each experience, she tries to remember that we 'cannot lose something or someone that was not ours to lose' and that 'this too shall pass'. As a mother of her seven-year-old daughter, she appreciates that some of the best moments in her life have been mentoring her daughter to a positive life and experiencing the countless playtime and adventures together. They continue building their strong bond with each other, with nature and with the source of life.

Luciane as a Speaker

Luciane Sperling is available as a keynote speaker, guest presenter or trainer/facilitator. She can speak about topics as:

- From Crisis to Blessings in 12 steps

- Bill of Rights for Women

- Questioning myself if I am in an abusive relationship – Now What?

- Youth Talk to Schools – (boys & girls)

Other speaking gigs upon request

Luciane would like to build a platform with programs to educate youth in the schools about abuse to protect their future relationships and create a better society. She believes that working from the 'seed' is the answer.

To request Luciane Sperling as a speaker and check her availability email: luciane@myinnerlight.com.au with subject line 'Speaking Request'. If perhaps you would like to request an interview, please write subject line 'Interview Request'.

Luciane has given interviews to Sydney Morning Herald, Channel 7 and local community/media: Please click the link below to watch them:

Video Channel 7 (3 June 2016)

- https://au.news.yahoo.com/video/watch/31761309/fo7-new-education-scheme-offers-abused-women-scholarships/?cmp=st#page1

Video Sydney Morning Herald Interview (30 June 2016)

- https://www.facebook.com/sydneymorningherald/videos/10154447539006264/

To order copies of *Touched by Love: Turning Crisis into a Blessing*, please use the following link: https://natasadenman.leadpages.co/touched-by-love-book/. If you would like to order a number of copies, please contact luciane@myinnerlight.com.au to receive a special discount.

Luciane's connections:

- Tafe Alumni member
- Ultimate Business Support – Natasa & Stuart Denman
- Member of Institute of Women International
- Member of Chertseydale Community Cottage
- Member of P&C Chertsey Primary School
- IWDA International Women's Development Agency
- Isagenix Australia
- League of Extraordinary Women
- Start Up Mum

- Working Mothers Connect
- WOW Wave of Wisdom

Thank you for buying and reading this book. By buying this book you will be supporting women and kids in need through different organisations Luciane likes to support.

- ✓ White Ribbon
- ✓ St Vincent de Paul Society
- ✓ The Salvation Army
- ✓ Coast Shelter
- ✓ Chertseydale Community Cottage
- ✓ Central Coast Family Support
- ✓ Central Coast Community Women's Health Centre
- ✓ Cancer Council NSW

Special Bonus

There is a special surprise gift to readers as my *thank you* for buying and reading this book. Please connect with me and it will be sent to you.

Website: (Please subscribe to receive your bonus)

www.myinnerlight.com.au

Email: (Talk to me)

luciane@myinnerlight.com.au

Facebook: Like 'My Inner Light' Facebook Page:

'My Inner Light' Facebook https://m.facebook.com/My-Inner-Light-1201584299855288

'Your task is not to seek love,
but to seek and find all the
barriers within yourself
that you have built
against it.'

– Rumi

www.ingramcontent.com/pod-product-compliance
Lightning Source LLC
Chambersburg PA
CBHW021125300426
44113CB00006B/288